Hand-Hewn

The Art of Building Your Own Cabin

by William C. Leitch

Chronicle Books

Line Drawings by Susan Leitch

A few years ago, the author instructed in a small experimental education program at a state university in the Northwest. To the students in that undertaking, who over the years pointed out new ways of "being in the world," this book is respectfully dedicated.

Copyright 1976 by William C. Leitch

Printed in the United States of America

Fourth Printing, December 1976

Library of Congress Cataloging in Publication Data

Leitch, William C
  Hand hewn: the art of building your own log cabin.

  1. Log cabins.   I. Title.
TH480.L44   694'.1   75-45418
ISBN 0-87701-079-X

Chronicle Books
870 Market Street
San Francisco, California 94102

Contents

To those who would look on such a project as a farce, or a chore not worth the time, we have little to say.
We speak instead to the individual who feels some loss in the realization that this age of miracles,
miraculous though it is, has robbed us of the need to use our hands . . . And we speak, in a sense,
to the child in man—that free spirit still building tree houses in the woods.
—FOXFIRE

Introduction

A hand-built log home is a unique structure, endowed with that rich mystery which envelops vast, silent forests everywhere. It is possessed of a magic which enchants and transforms those who would build it. It gently imposes a way of life on its builders, a way of life which is today being accepted with relief by an ever-increasing number of people.

Those who have built log cabins have found that the experience is somehow much more than the mere construction of a funky shelter or the acquiring of skill in a particular craft. The activities involved in the project— the acquisition of the land, the gathering of materials, the move into the woods, the construction of the cabin itself—become a profound educational experience. The builders are afforded a glimpse of a tantalizingly different way of living in the world, a different means of personal and social self-actualization.

As an effective educational experience changes the behavior of the student, an effective log cabin experience changes the behavior of its builder. The experience is made rich not simply by the careful placement of one log atop another, but also by the dreams and anticipations, the designing and execution of plans, and the rediscovery of neglected virtues—self-reliance and creative resourcefulness. This book is concerned as much with these aspects of the log cabin as with its construction.

The resurgence of interest in log construction is to some extent a fad. History's marvelous twists and turns have converted the log structure into a status symbol. In many parts of the country, it is "in" to have a log home. The rich have them. But the new interest is also a response, especially by the young, to recent political, economic, and educational conditions, as well as to the arid and sterile state of modern housing. It is a revolt by those who have realized that long-term mortgages are neither necessary nor desirable features of twentieth-century life, and by those who have rediscovered that they can provide themselves with adequate shelter with their own hands.

In an earlier day, those who chose to settle in the mountains and forests had no choice but to create their shelter from the raw materials around them. Out of this necessity, by way of Northern Europe, grew the New World tradition of log construction. Today, it is no longer *necessary* to use raw materials as they come from the forests. Many of those forests have succumbed to industry's insatiable appetites and many other modes of construction are now available to the home-builder. Shelter may be provided quickly, though not cheaply; it will be adequate, though not enduring. Seldom is the shelter beautiful, rarely is it aesthetically satisfying. And, almost invariably, someone else experiences the pleasure of creating the home one inhabits.

There was bound to be a reaction.

Today, a rapidly burgeoning group of people, no longer impelled by necessity, is returning to the mountains, to log construction, and to many of the tradition-imparted values associated with log cabins. These structures, along with the love, thought, and work that goes into them, are extensions of their inhabitants and tacitly express an attitude toward modern society. This book therefore focuses its attention on recent log construction, in the hope of capturing and passing on to others some of this present-day spirit.

The illustrations—intended to stimulate imagination, rather than to copy—have been selected from the Western Rockies because here many of these people have discovered their "sense of place." This log work is from widely-scattered parts of Wyoming, Idaho, Montana, Washington and British Columbia. But, whatever the poitical subdivision, in these mountains are forests, and scattered through them are those people who have quite literally *made* their homes there.

The builders of this house truly love wild, growing things.

1

Mountains: On Being There

From without: The crisp clarity of icy winter nights. Short quiet walks through deeply shaded spring-green groves. Scum ice hissing down the streambed. The long steady climb to alpine meadows and the binocular survey of the mountainsides. The sharp odor of dislodged granite and the sharp marmot whistle. Phlox, mountain sorrel, and paintbrush. Muffled, silent snowfalls.

From within: Wholeness. A Zen-like total immersion in the hand construction of a home. The deep contentment evoked by serene, natural surroundings. Good health, good appetite, good lovemaking. An alerted sense of participation in primeval natural processes and cycles. The palpable sense of good neighborliness. Quiet.

These are firm realities, which mountain dwellers experience through the seasons in their daily lives. Such experiences are within everyone's reach, yet few people choose to live in the mountains.

Why? The obvious drawbacks are climate, relative isolation, and economics. But the more critical factors are human characteristics, and less obvious: a vague sense of personal inadequacy, confusion over social obligations, and spirit-crushing inertia.

Let us look more closely at each of these factors.

Despite their fierce reputations, most mountain climates are relatively mild. Summer thunderstorms bring frequent rain, and winter, of course, means deep snow. Transportation becomes difficult, but not impossible, especially since the advent of snow machines. The sustained subzero cold snaps which settle over the Northern Great Plains are relatively uncommon in major mountain chains, even though mean annual temperatures are lower in the mountains. The interaction of mountain climate and vegetation does produce hordes of insects which prey on soft-skinned man, however, and which quickly discourage the visitor unused to their merciless appetites.

The harshest weather, of course, has its positive side. Before the snow has fallen for long, you will be rummaging around for your ski boots, mittens and waxes. This is also the time when large mammals move down into the valleys. With some practice, you will find that their tracks in the snow provide a vivid tableau of the wildlife that shares your neighborhood and will reveal some of their activities.

The most successful mountain dwellers seem to be those who have miraculously turned those characteristics of the mountains which seem to most people to be negative—rugged terrain, snow, ice, cold—to their leisure advantage. Snow is not merely that substance which makes the peaks more beautiful than usual. It provides new activities. It is cherished and experienced. Those who are forced indoors by inclement weather soon become bored and restless victims of cabin fever.

The isolation which most people ascribe to mountain life can be a positive or negative attribute, depending upon one's point of view. Social intercourse is quantitatively reduced, it is true, but it is usually qualitatively enhanced. The increase in human activity demanded by the elements is shared by all. Work parties are common. Books and tools are shared. One visits a friend not merely for entertainment, but to warm up for a bit, or to help out, or for news of the neighborhood. Lack of intellectual stimulation is a frequent complaint, yet the

curiosity which underlies it, wherever one is, origi-
nates, after all, from within. Ultimately, each person
provides his own best intellectual stimulation.

Isolation as a negative attribute usually means a lack
of that frenetic, electronic glee we call entertainment,
which all too often leaves in its wake a vapid, hollow
after-effect. Most of what today is called fun is activity
which puts us into the passive role of observer: movies,
spectator sports, bars, television, even some parties.
The activity ends, and with it, the fun. In the mountains,
however, we can enjoy participatory activities alone
or in good company: fishing, building, backpacking,
horseback riding. We love to fish because we are parti-
cipants, not mere observers. When the fishing ends, the
fun lingers because the experience has become a part of
us.

Major among the drawbacks of mountain life is the
difficulty of earning a living there. You may find yourself among the ranks of the very poor. Such a prospect
can not be shrugged off, for the reckoning will finally
arrive, and if you have not faced the problem squarely
you will become a burden upon your friends and
neighbors. Savings will dwindle. Death and taxes are
still certain. The adjustment to bare subsistence can be
difficult, particularly for those who have enjoyed relative affluence. But the uncertainty of income should not
deter you absolutely, for the mountains invariably teach
their new inhabitants a vital lesson in economics: when
you live outside, or on the fringe of orthodox energy
networks, a little cash goes a long way, and the quality
of your life need not deteriorate. This fact has helped
many people to solve the income problem in a variety of
ways. Some people work for wages for a few months of
the year, and don't work at all (for money) during the
remaining months. Others alternate a full year of cash-
earning with a full year of mountain life. Still others
collectivize or communalize their lives in the mountains, sharing resources, skills, and labor, thereby reducing the requirements of each individual or family

unit. By necessity, vocations are often dramatically
changed. Executives or professionals may find themselves punching cows or herding sheep; academicians
may find themselves grappling with the more mundane
and concrete problems of planting trees or fighting fires.
The willingness to take up unfamiliar tasks is a reliable
indicator of success in cabin building or life in the mountains.

Mountain life is rigorous. The amount of time that
basic maintenance chores demand is astounding. Provision of wood for heating and cooking will occupy several days of each year and cannot be ignored. Casual
visitors seldom notice that far more discipline is required in the daily business of mountain life than in
almost any other living conditions. The more discerning
realize that wood must be chopped, water carried, gardens tended, kindling split, animals fed, dishes washed.
These visitors therefore pitch in to help. They are always welcomed back.

Many people are prevented from moving into the high
country by a sense of personal inadequacy. They fear
that they would not be able to develop the skills or
marshal the resources necessary for the move. I can only
repeat that no special talents or qualifications are required for these skills and resources that must eventually
be acquired other than an open mind, patience, and an
aversion to the herd.

Confusion over social obligations plagues many of
those who would move to the mountains. Those whose
politics are strident and emphatic often view mountain
life as a cop-out, an evasion of social responsibility. Yet
many of the cabins illustrated in this book were built in
the Canadian Rockies by men and women who have
paid the heavy price of exile for refusing to compromise
their social principles. Their motives are beyond re-
proach. Some consider themselves to be refugees, but
few consider themselves escapists.

The hardest problems to solve are always those you
create yourself. And your perception of your social ob-

A simple, attractive porch design. Note the palisaded log section beneath the window.

ligations may occupy your thoughts for years before you resolve the questions to your own satisfaction.

It is vital, however, even if you cannot come up with immediate answers, to ask yourself these questions before you move to the mountains:

Must I be in close touch with modern society in order to participate in its improvement?

Can I honestly justify my own possession of a lifestyle denied, for whatever reason, to others?

Should my taking up of a simple, active life be part of a collective, communal effort?

Have I the strength to recognize wealth, status, and the possession of materials beyond my reasonable needs as false gods?

Is my envisioned style of life revolutionary or reactionary? Conservative or radical? Will I transcend labels such as these?

You will recognize these questions as anthropocentric, even egocentric. You also need to ask questions with implications beyond the man-centered ones, developing an ability to see yourself as part of an interrelated and interdependent ecosystem. For instance, what will be the effects of your incursion into the habitat of local wildlife?

Your answers to these and similar questions will help you to determine your own suitability for life in the mountains. Rarely will such questions evoke simple yes or no answers. If such questions have already occurred to you, they will not remain behind while you go to the mountains. The only logic which will help you once you have moved to the mountains is the inexorable logic of natural forces, which clears the muddiest waters. The historical determinist, frozen into his dogma, will answer one way; the flower child, enraptured by notions of the noble savage, will answer another way. Neither is likely to be happy for long in the mountains . . .

The factor which probably keeps most people from living in the mountains is simply inertia: the disinclination to move or act. It is easy to mistake a steady income, a secure social position, or assured career advancement for life's deeper promises. Even when we know better, we usually choose the safer, tangible rewards and put off seeking richer rewards until "later."

There is no easy formula for overcoming inertia. Some people manage it by accident; they visit a friend in the mountains and find that they like it there. Some are moved by force of circumstance; they lose their job and a planned mountain interim becomes permanent. A few act by design; they collect their courage, arrange their affairs, and move. For all, good luck plays a part.

If you move to the mountains and construct your own home, there is a real possibility that you will be led into a new and different lifestyle, well clear of the roaring mainstream of modern western civilization.

There is fear involved, and risk. But there is also the potential for salvation, sanity, and increased awareness of self and society.

Palisaded logs form the first floor walls of this storybook house.

2

The New Pioneers

We were not seeking to escape. Quite the
contrary, we wanted to find a way in which we
could put more into life and get more out of it.
—HELEN AND SCOTT NEARING

I do not think that any civilization can be
called complete until it has progressed from
sophistication to unsophistication, and
made a conscious return to simplicity
of thinking and living.
—LIN YUTANG

For those poised on the verge of a new life—those who
are not sure they could or should build their own cabin
—a generalized profile of those who have already taken
the plunge may help.

Scores of motives have sent builders into the woods
with axes, chain saws, and new visions during the past
decade. Most are outright or implicit rebels. Some flee
to the woods, appalled by civilization, others are drawn
by what is already there, or by what they hope to create
there. A few bring with them what they had intended to
leave behind, and are disappointed.

Most of them are outraged by the war, ultra-
specialization, corrupt government, superficial life
styles, environmental degradation, and the alienating
labor of a materially-oriented society. They have not
chosen to escape these problems, but rather to engage
them on different terms, within a context they have
themselves created.

A few have fled, without apology, from broken mar-
riages, mindless jobs, frenetic cities, hang-ups with
family and friends, or simply because they can not function satisfactorily within a modern mass society.

What characteristics do these people share?

Youthful, restless exuberance. They enjoy themselves immensely. You don't often meet them today in
casual society, although the turmoils of the last decade
have increased their numbers appreciably, because they
are either deep in their woods or traveling in strange and
wondrous lands (Patagonia, The Barren Grounds,
Nepal). We are acquainted with those who have dropped
out and into Marrakesh, Haight-Ashbury, Katmandu,
Goa, Boulder, and Vancouver. But those who have

dropped out and into Alaska, rural British Columbia,
Montana, and Idaho are well out of sight and determined
to stay that way. Indeed, anonymity is a frequent pre-
requisite to an interview or photograph. They may be of
any age but their attitudes toward themselves, others,
and their surroundings are *never* rigid, a quality usually
attributed to the young.

Contempt for wealth. They are not affluent and have
little interest in becoming so. They travel cheaply. Their
needs are few. For most of them, wealth represents
neither real security nor an amibition worthy of great
effort.

Regard for wildlife. With very few exceptions, they
are lovers of wildlife. *All* wildlife, not just deer, bear
and elk. They are acquainted with and frequently
knowledgeable about the flowers, grasses, and trees in
their area, and know the habits of local ground squirrels,
mice and voles, birds, etc. Their libraries include guides
and keys to regional flora and fauna. For these people,
the presence or absence of flourishing wildlife popula-
tions is a prime factor in determining selection of a cabin
site.

Energy. They have energy in abundance. They are
seldom cabinbound for long, even in deepest winter,
and they tend to hike rather than stroll. When they work
on their cabins, twelve-hour days are not uncommon.
High energy leisure activities are a common characteristic.

Solitude. A few must have utter solitude and thus live
far from populated areas because they can not easily find
others who can competently share their life style. For
most, peace, quiet, and solitude are recurrent require-

The large, paired windows, log porch, and second story balcony give this house a distinctive style.

ments. They cannot live comfortably in an environment which denies these requirements absolutely.

Regard for mountains. In most respects, life is easier outside the mountains. Yet most of these people would not dream of living elsewhere. In an ecological sense, many of their habitat requirements are provided by mountainous country. The mountains provide low population densities, high-energy recreation opportunities, the raw materials for their shelters, relatively abundant wildlife, low pollution levels, and the extremes of weather and climate which they cherish. Not all life-support systems are provided, however. Jobs are scarce in the mountains, so these people often work part of the year elsewhere, since it is usually necessary for them to work for wages. Complete self-subsistence is rare, for the rigors of montane climates and the acidic forest soils often preclude rich gardens or cash-crop tillage. Thus, love of mountains distinguishes these people from the more familiar back-to-the-landers, who seek above all rich soil and benign climate. In their hierarchy of values, mountains come first, gardens much later.

Craftsmanship. A commonly shared characteristic is that of working skillfully with one's hands. This tendency extends to the cabin work, or course, but there are usually other areas of endeavor which require some form of craftsmanship. Some tie flies, others do their own leather work, or string snowshoes, sew their own camping gear, or build furniture. This habit seems to stem from a reaction to our highly technologized "ready-made" society, but also represents a frank recognition of the importance of self-reliance. Very few become "gadgeteers," encumbered with the latest devices for back-packing or mountain-climbing. Most are self-taught craftsmen.

Outdoors activities. These men and women tend to be active and skilled outdoorsmen. They hike in the summer, snowshoe and ski in the winter, frequently alone. When time and money are available, they may drive hundreds of miles to backpack in a promising area, but they usually spend most of their outdoor time near their cabin. The immediate outdoor environment is, after all one of the primary criteria for their selection of home-site.

The builders of the cabins illustrated here come from diverse backgrounds. Their educations, and political and philosophical complexions vary widely. But all face the problem of how to stay where they are. They view with apprehension the steady encroachment of those whose attachment to land is tenuous at best.

Above all, they take pride in their craft.

This complex log building was designed and constructed by one man. The versatility of logs as a building material is unmatched for imaginative craftsmen.

3

Myths and Strategies

There is some of the same fitness in a man's
building his own house that there is in a bird's
building its own nest.
—HENRY DAVID THOREAU

The novice must overcome several myths which tenaciously embrace the idea of building your own log home, often intimidating those who would build their home by hand, and frightening them away from the project. Some of these myths derive from aspects of the pioneer tradition which cling to log construction, but which no longer obtain in 1975 North America. Others are husbanded, no doubt unwittingly, by log specialists whose professions are enhanced by specialized knowledge.

The experienced builder, on the other hand, takes with him into the woods certain strategies with respect to log cabins. These strategies tend to maximize satisfaction and minimize cost. Sometimes they are well thought out, carefully considered strategies; more often they are vague, but compelling notions of how to approach the upcoming job. They bring about shelter which is well-designed, well-built, and relatively inexpensive.

Let's consider some of these myths, and see if we can lay them to rest, replacing them with positive strategies.

Myth 1: *You can't do it alone.*

You *can* do it alone, because thousands of people with far less strength, imagination, or education than you possess have done it in the past and will do it in the future. You *shouldn't* do it alone, though, because it's selfish not to share all that pleasure. Get somebody to help you and you won't need to do it alone. (You will find, however, as my wife and I did, that too much help, when you needed to rest or think, is a much more serious problem than not enough help.) If you insist on working by yourself, or if circumstances require it, you still needn't fear having to rent or buy expensive machinery

to lift your logs for you. You will be astounded at the weight you can maneuver alone if you take time to experiment. There is a limit, of course, which you will eventually find, and you then scale your design accordingly. The solution may be as simple as using shorter, lighter logs.

Myth 2: *You can't do it because you don't know anything about it.*

The most frequent comments by those who visited our log home during various phases of construction ran like this: "I've always wanted to do something like this, but I'd never be able to," or "Far out! I wish I could do this," or "Where'd you get the courage to do this?" or "I didn't know you guys were carpenters." (One of the "guys" standing there is my petite wife.) There's a widespread impression that one must be a carpenter, architect, North Woods trapper, in possession of ancient secrets, or some combination of these in order to build his own log home. Yet none of the homes illustrated in this book were built by carpenters-in-trade, trappers, or architects. Very few of the builders were skilled wood-workers *when they started*. But, through on-the-job training, most of them were rather skilled craftsmen when they finished their homes. Logs are very kind to novices: they are tolerant of, and even hide mistakes. Division of labor along sexual lines is nearly meaningless; there are few times when raw strength is required, and a diminutive, careful girl wielding a double-bitted cruising axe will hew a much better round notch than a sloppy or impatient man.

Some log homes, of course, are conceived, erected, and finished with more skill and with higher standards of craftsmanship than others. But a home of nearly any

Two men constructed this home.

standard of log-craftsmanship will support life and provide adequate shelter, warmth, and satisfaction.

Myth 3: *You can build your log home nearly free.*

No, you can't. The main investment is time, which is well rewarded. But you will have to spend some money—for land, tools, food to keep you while you're building, materials you can't scrounge, beer on a hot day. The logs alone, it is true, won't cost you much. If they are from your own land, they will be free. If you buy them from the Forest Service, as do most builders, they will cost from fifty to three hundred dollars.

Strategy 1: *You can build your own log home with your own hands and mind.*

Consider birds. Every year they undertake to build their own homes, without instruction. They work hard and make skillful uses of their local resources. Their nest is adequate to their needs—it must be—and it usually blends in marvelously with its immediate surroundings. It belongs. The materials are free. Birds frequently have a very nice view. One imagines that they have pride in their craftsmanship.

Why should you settle for less?

One may think, ". . . but their materials are free." Nest-building materials are generally the cast-off remnants of a bird's surroundings: twigs, leaves, bits of hair and fur, dry moss. Our human society discards, in great abundance, materials we can use in providing our shelter. When humans no longer need a building, they simply abandon it or pay someone to take it down, brick by brick, board by board, and dispose of it. Here lie our free materials.

"But," you may object, "they, after all, are birds. I'm a human being, thoughtful, with history and memory and ambitions and problems to solve." Be thankful for it, for you don't face the ever present problem of becoming something's dinner, or getting caught in a late snowstorm, or contracting a disease and receiving no medication, or becoming the target of hunters or thoughtless children.

Nevertheless, the basic problems we face are essentially the same as those faced by birds: maintenance and survival. The difference between birds and ourselves is that while they are instinctively singleminded about solving these problems, we are not. They demonstrate great efficiency; *every* effort is directed toward maintenance and survival. We, on the other hand, must have our second cars, our trips to Europe, our promotions, our color televisions.

Nature is exceedingly harsh in her treatment of those of her charges who are grossly inefficient. We therefore pay for our profligacy with ulcers, angina pectoris, ennui, and barbaric conflicts amongst ourselves. The ultimate price may be premature extinction.

While we can't sprout wings and feathers—nor should we, were some magic transformation possible —we *do* have our own unfathomable niche. We possess the capacity to become benign, useful members of the community of living things on our planet.

The strategy of building one's own home requires above all a confident frame of mind. The birds put their eons of accumulated instinct to work to complete their nests. We, instinct-shorn by our "higher civilization," must replace it with confidence. Every successful log builder takes this confidence into the woods with him, and it is the confidence, working out through mind and body, which completes the structure.

It is possible to build log homes with little other than sweat, tools, and time.

Strategy 2. *You can solve all of the problems and do all of the jobs relating to building and finishing your own log home.*

As you reflect on your project you quickly realize that you need some of the knowledge of a plumber, carpenter, mason, roofer, geologist, logger, artist, mathematician, and painter, to name but a few. A scary list. But you really only need a small amount of each skill in order to meet a criterion of adequacy. You will find that various skills will accrue in stages, as the need for them develops. Sure, the pipes may leak at first, but having put them in, you now know how to fix them. Contemporary society's emphasis on division of labor has conditioned us in such a way that, when we encounter a new problem, our first inclination is to call a "specialist" in to solve it for us, rather than to bend our own mind to the task at hand. One needn't rediscover the principles of hydraulic mechanics in order to build a proper spring box, or to run water into the kitchen.

Strategy 3. *You can make carefully considered use of machines to assist you in your labors.*

I know some people who will not permit any machines to be brought onto their land, much less allow their use in construction. They limit their experience by failure to adapt technology to humane use, while avoiding its oppressive employment. Others I've met will use every machine they can buy or borrow whenever possible. This second group does not reap the full satisfaction that working with one's hands yields.

The machines that you would be most likely to employ in log construction—assuming that there is no electricity on your site—are vehicles (for skidding logs, transporting materials, going fishing), winches (for raising heavy logs high), and that most controversial object, the chain saw. Today, almost everybody uses vehicles and people can usually do what a winch can do—it just takes longer. The heavy arguments are over the chain saw.

If you are an environmentalist of the purest strain and have plenty of time—it also helps to have a favorable climate—don't use a chain saw. But if your land is without electricity you will probably use wood for cooking and heating fuel. If you are poor, you will certainly be using wood, and you will need a chain saw.

It is only proper to have doubts about using a very loud, fossil fuel-consuming machine which is used widely to destroy forests like the one around you. Remember, though, that blame for the nightmarish aspects of modern technology is borne not by the machines themselves, but by those who wield them. The use to which you will put the saw is creative, not destructive. You will discover soon that there are many sawing jobs that it will not do. It will not release you from all toil. You will still drip hot sweat into your logs.

By ingenious use of the "gin pole" and a system of pulleys and cables, this builder has been able to move large logs without any assistance.

Strategy 4. *You can manufacture most, but not all of your building materials.*

If you intend to build your cabin cheaply and yet to construct a solid structure that will last for several generations, do not visit your local lumber yard, submit your materials list, and ask for delivery as soon as possible. Your materials will be adequate and your cabin may endure, but it will certainly not be cheap. If, on the other hand, you decide to saw all of your planks by hand, to hand-split your roof shakes, and to forge your own hinges and latches, your grandchildren are likely to be your cabin's first inhabitants. I advocate a strategy somewhere between these extremes. To be sure, you will have to purchase some items from your local lumber yard, but an incredible amount of material is available to you free or nearly free if you will take the time to seek it out. Further, if you exercise your imagination, you will find countless ways to utilize the log-ends, short log sections, poles, and other by-products left over from the major construction job when finishing your house.

Strategy 5. *You can build this home, even if you cannot commit your full life to it now.*

Few of the homes in this book were built when the builder was able to devote full time to it. They were constructed during summer vacations, weekends, after work. They got worked on when the owners could find the time, money, or frame of mind to proceed. If you say to youself, "I'll wait until I can do this full time," you run the grave risk of never doing any of it. Face the facts. No matter how well things look now, something will come up; you'll have a baby, or another baby, or wreck your car, or be asked to join in yet another of our wars. So don't put it off. Start your efforts to build this home right now. Once started, the cabin will begin to exert its magic upon you and yours, and will become a persistent factor in major life decisions.

Strategy 6. *You will be able to finish your log home within one or two summers.*

It is true that you may be able to build, and move into your cabin with your basic needs provided for, within one or two years of part-time work. Many manage this in one summer. But try to avoid thinking in terms of completely finishing the job. One of the profound lessons the log cabin will teach you is that most of the satisfaction to be gained, the lessons to be learned, are in the constructing of it, not in the completing of it. Once it is finally completed, the bell has rung, class is over. Don't worry, though, for there are always those little tasks you weren't able to get to before. There are out-buildings, and perhaps more cabins to be built. But most important, by now your log cabin has changed your life, and there are new discoveries to be made, new lessons to be learned.

Strategy 7. *You will recognize that building your own log home is an exercise in self-discovery.*

Building is a creative act, a means of expression which allows us to clearly measure our daily accomplishments and, if we have worked well, to take pride in the day's work. It is labor which returns meaning to each day, labor which fatigues rather than frustrates, and leads to deep, healing sleep. Building with logs is hard labor, but not meaningless toil. Your appetite will be hearty; you will eat well to keep up your strength. You will discover some new limits and realize some new potentials.

4

We are all living *off* the land, no matter where
and how we do it. The possibility of living
with the land is also open.
—**DAVID LANGSNER**

Why Logs?

Modern technology and the advertising which serve it have led most of us so far from using our own hands that we are usually appalled at the prospect of doing so. Especially if we use an unfamiliar construction medium, such as logs, for our shelter.

Prior to the arrival of the logs for our own cabin, my wife and I were confident and eager to get started with the work. The day finally arrived when a huge cloud of dust appeared to the North and from it materialized a logging truck loaded with ninety-four large, long, heavy-looking logs. The trucker asked where we wanted them and we indicated a clear space among the willows in the creek bottom. He pulled up, got out of his truck, attached some cable to some pins, stood well back, and jerked hard. With a great roar, the logs tumbled off the truck. Bark and sod flew in every direction, and the whole works settled into a crazed and jumbled pile resembling a giant's fresh-tossed game of pick-up-sticks. The logger turned his truck around and roared off in the midst of another dust cloud, leaving us to survey our raw materials in depressed silence. Somehow we had not anticipated this gigantic tangle of heavy logs, seemingly interlocked and pinned at every point.

Dark doubts crowded in upon us. How were we to sort them, as the books tell us to do? How could we move them to our cabin site, two hundred feet away? Had our reach too far over exceeded our grasp? At that moment, after years of dreaming and months of planning, the thought surfaced, "Why the hell logs?"

Well, we did sort them out, and with the help of cant hooks, cables, and poles for levers, grew skilled at removing the precise logs we needed. As the pile diminished, so did our doubts.

Building your own shelter of any sort will satisfy some deepseated needs. Any structure you work on will provide you with some sense of creative accomplishment. Your work will tend to affirm your worth as a craftsman, as one who can recognize a problem, engage it, and resolve it. The experience of building your shelter with your own hands may not solve your existential dilemmas overnight, but it certainly creates the satisfying illusion that you are the master over a small part of your destiny. *Any* structure—dome or zome, yurt or tepee—will offer such rewards, provided that you build it yourself.

But log work adds a dimension to these rewards which is not easily satisfied by work with other construction materials, except perhaps adobe. On aesthetic grounds, the log cabin is one of those rare man-made shelters which looks like it "belongs" in its surroundings. So compelling is this concordance between log cabin and forest that a cabin situated in a non-forested site loses this architectural elegance as if by witchcraft. Old log cabins found empty on the back roads of the great plains (to which early settlers had to bring their logs dozens or scores of miles from the nearest forests) have a stark and eerie quality about them. They appear to have intruded. Log cabins belong in forests, and are ill-suited to the eye elsewhere.

There are strong ecological grounds for working with logs. Like, no waste. When you peel the logs, the bark strips go over the garden as mulch, or when sun-dried, into the wood-box as excellent kindling. The sawdust goes to the cat-box or chicken coop. Chips from the axe-work warm your supper in the wood stove. Those short sections you cut out for windows and doors become counter supports, table legs, or staircase parts. Nothing is wasted. The knottiest, twistiest piece will

king aspens and an unusually designed cabin.

This house was built from telephone pole ends. Note the use of half-poles for porch flooring.

find a use somewhere, even if only to go into the stove. The log cabin is the ultimate recyclable house. Given proper construction and a modicum of maintenance, a log cabin will last for several generations, but if it is deserted it will eventually return gently to the earth, leaving no trace behind save a grass-shrouded foundation. Its organic constituents are broken down quickly into their inorganic elements, and rejoin the cycle eternal. Thus a log cabin is an eminently appropriate use of a living, renewable resource. Few of its structural elements need to have been pumped from oil wells, distilled from petroleum, or boiled in electrolytic baths.

While only the bravest and most ingenious of us can provide log cabins for ourselves at no cost, they are nevertheless well-suited for those of us who have more time than money. The construction of a log house need not condemn us to the bondage of a twenty-year mortgage. The avoidance of such subjugation is indeed one of the most urgent reasons for building with logs. For economic reasons, the best logs for cabin construction are not necessarily the best from which to cut lumber. Therefore, even those forests which have been ruthlessly exploited for the lumber market can produce logs for cabin construction in abundance. Forests are generous with their bounty, and provide well for those who treat them with respect, moderation, and reverence.

Even with all these advantages, it is an ironic fact that many people are afraid to attempt to construct their homes with logs. Something akin to fear of being old-fashioned, or of dawdling away time better spent elsewhere grips them, and the whole point is thus missed. Yet in most respects, no special skills are required which can not be learned *during the actual cabin building*. The labor involved is satisfying because it calls for the integration of body and mind, not the dis-integration of mind and body upon which modern industry depends. The few tools which must be mastered require the concerted effort of mind, body, and eye.

Log cabins readily forgive us our initial lack of skill. If you live in Brooklyn, Omaha, or San Jose, and have never handled an axe, don't worry about it, for you will soon learn. If you don't know how to move a forty-foot, three-hundred pound log to the top of a twelve-foot wall, don't give up. It's unlikely that you've ever had to solve such problems in the past, so of course you regard them somewhat fearfully. Much to your surprise, you will be able to do it. You have the thinking apparatus and the strength required to solve this problem. Most of the construction work can be done by one person, if plenty of time is allowed for. Two persons can do virtually any work associated with the cabin. Thought, not brute strength, achieves the most difficult tasks involved.

Finally, if you build a log cabin, you employ a construction material which is easily "worked." If you want a nail somewhere, you simply drive one in. If you change your mind later, you pull it out, and the nail-hole nearly vanishes. If you can't stand metal, you drill a hole, carve a peg to fit it, and pound it in. If you need to level off a wall, you make your measurement, snap a chalk-line, and hew the log down to your line. If you decide that you need an additional window in the bedroom after most of the house is built, just take some structural precautions and cut it out. Few building materials will tolerate such treatment and allow such latitude as logs.

When you are nearly ready to move into your cabin and you let your mind wander back through memories of cabin building, you will realize that what those logs provided in greatest measure was deep satisfaction. And therein lies the answer to the question, why logs?

You will no doubt have occasion to use a hammer and chisel to cut out some special support notch. The day will be warm and still, a few flies buzz, the sun will be hot on your bare shoulders as you sit . . . tap, tap, tap. You try to fit the board into the notch. Still too small. Tap, tap. Try it again for fit. This time it slides smoothly into place. You gently tap it with the hammer until it is snug and flush. A perfect fit! You get up, go over to the water jug sitting in the shade and take a long, icy pull. You look down the meadow for deer. None. You look up the hillside to see if eagles are riding the updrafts, looking for scrambling ground squirrels. Not today. Then your eye is irresistably drawn back to the newly-finished notch. You go back over to it, rub your hand along the joint, and think to yourself, "How about that. A perfect fit." Then you move on to the next job, satisfied.

You have just experienced a Michelangelo rush. The master could not have experienced much more sheer exhiliration at work well done than you just have. You celebrate, for a brief moment, the successful collaboration of hand and eye. For that moment, you and your work are one—whole.

Clearly, all jobs involved in building your cabin will not be so richly rewarding. If you merely subjugate a construction medium (in this case, logs) to your technological prowess, force the fit amidst the roar and fumes of the chain saw, you may glance back again, but you will not admire. By now you know the difference between self-indulgence and the legitimate satisfaction that derives from the use of your own creative, intellec-tual, and slowly developing physical resources to solve a construction problem. The quality of the work depends in part upon the attitude you have toward it. The distinction between work well done and work done poorly is often subtle, even when the net result of the two jobs is the same. But as the experiences arise, you will instantly distinguish between the two qualities.

If you have recognized the potential horrors of the machine age, and if you are increasingly cautious and thoughtful about ushering yourself rapturously into the technological future, you will derive some pleasure from veering slightly away from that course. Some among you will consider yourselves anchorites, refugees from modern society, and you will doubtless deny yourselves many of the tools created since the industrial revolution. Your road is long, steep, and lonely.

Much of the satisfaction you receive from building a log cabin defies analysis. You solve problems through your own effort, you become one with that effort, you suffer the despair and the ecstasy of creation through it. You are a human being, alive, with a home to build. That joy will not be denied.

5

The Cabin Journal

A cabin journal can be your most valuable tool. Well before you begin construction, while your log cabin is yet a faint glimmer on the periphery of your daydreams, while you are awaiting the right frame of mind, or later, when you are searching for land, or gathering building materials—as early as possible—begin to keep a cabin journal. It is important to start early, for one of its main functions is to reflect for you the *approach* to your project.

The day will eventually arrive when you will wonder how you could have gotten along without it. The journal provides a center, a point of reference from which to judge the effects of your new activity upon your life. It is the tablet upon which the milestones are etched.

It is the most versatile tool you can employ, for it puts your mind, sense, and body to work. It makes you *think,* and helps you to *see.*

If you are reasonably diligent about writing in it, your cabin journal will reflect the ups and downs, but will smooth them out, and in time will give you a long and comforting look back into the history of you and your cabin.

It will record high-flying days and wretched bummers:

"18 February. Noon temperature: 15°. Weather: clear and cold. A fine day. We walked through crisp snow for the last mile or so. Down by the lower homestead we saw two small herds of does and several antelope. Near the upper home-stead we saw a lot of deer and elk (looked like it) tracks from the beaver ponds on up to the old bridge. We didn't see anything, but a snowmobiler said there was an elk herd just over the ridge in the middle fork. As we came back along the creek it looked as if the beavers were coming out of the water

to cut willows. There is a three-foot drift in front of the new cabin and none in front of the old one. The spring and creek are open and running. The weather is much more pleasant than I expected for 7000 feet of elevation. This place is so relaxing compared to the pace of the city. I don't realize how much pressure there is until I come here and unwind!"

"10 July. Hot and still. The horse flies and deer flies are now joining the mosquitos. I picked a tick off my arm to-night. That's the second. I dropped one end of a log off the west wall, and it knocked a hole in the subfloor. We ran out of milk and gas for the lantern, and Kelly came home tonight with his nose and front paws full of porcupine quills. Jesus!"

The journal may serve simultaneously as a budget ledger, materials list, index of comparative prices, memory jogger, timetable, sketch book, and planning portfolio. If you record weather information at your site, your journal will begin to teach you the details of the ebb and flow of the seasons. Soon you'll know when to expect the first blades of grass, the first mosquitos and salmonflies, the first frost and last snowfall. And when you begin to build, milestone days will be recorded for your future reminiscences—not just raising the ridgepole, but finishing the foundation, hewing your first notch, gloating over perfectly level walls, and discovering how slippery wet logs are. All of this slowly accumulated information will have more practical application than may at first be apparent. If you are a fly fisherman, you will know when to take dry flies with you, and when nymphs. Wildlife watchers will be impatiently awaiting the first sparrow hawks or the awkward magpie fledglings, and will learn when to expect the ground squirrels to emerge and head for the garden. The clever gardeners among you will learn not to plant seeds

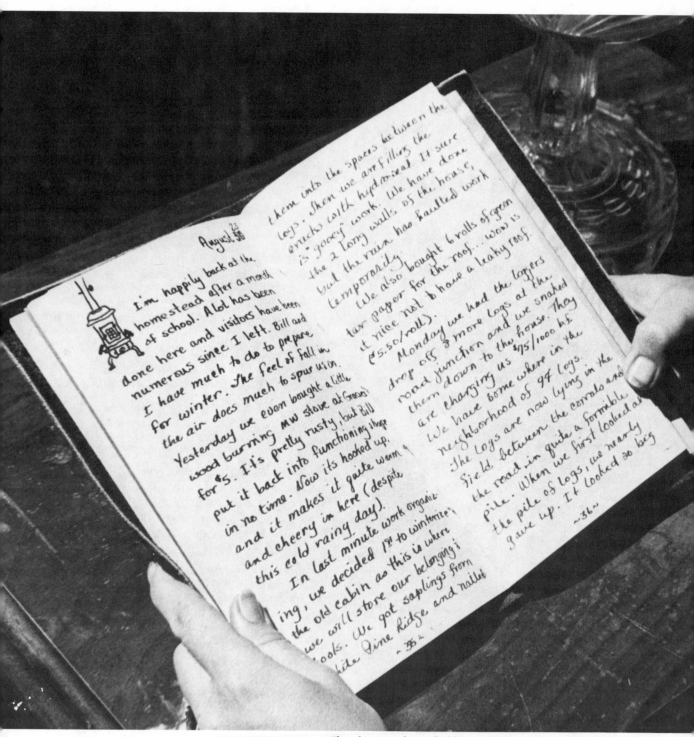

August 23

I'm happily back at the homestead after a month at school. A lot has been done here and visitors have been numerous since I left. Bill and I have much to do to prepare for winter. The feel of fall in the air does much to spur us in.

Yesterday we even bought a little wood burning mw stove at Green's for $5. It's pretty rusty, but Bill put it back into functioning shape in no time. Now its hooked up, and it makes it quite warm and cheery in here (despite this cold raing day).

In last minute work organiz- ing, we decided 1st to winterize the old cabin as this is where we will store our belongings & tools. We got saplings from ...ite Pine Ridge and nailt

~35~

them into the spaces between the logs. Then we are filling the cracks with hydromeal. It sure is gooey work. We have done the 2 long walls of the house, but the rain has hauled work temporarily.

We also bought 6 rolls of green tar paper for the roof... wow is it nice not to have a leaky roof ($5.50/roll).

Monday we had the loggers drop off 8 more logs at the road junction and we snaked them down to the house. They are charging us $75/1000 b.f. We have somewhere in the neighborhood of 98 logs. The logs are now lying in the field between the corrals and the road in quite a formidable pile. When we first looked at the pile of logs, we nearly gave up. It looked so big.

~36~

The cabin journal—a valuable record before, during and after construction.

too early. A journal with lots of rainy day entries may suggest a particular roof construction to you, or teach you to budget your time and plan activities in accordance with the weather. Snowy entries will hint at careful insulation. Mosquito entries inevitably suggest screens.

Make your journal, among other things, into a repository of local know-how, particularly with respect to weather, local resources, economic activities (logging, mining, ranching, etc.), as well as local history and customs. Your closest neighbors may, for example, be able to tell you that the ground freezes to about a foot in depth during the coldest winters, and save you having to dig a deep foundation. They may be able to tell you about an abandoned sawmill which is strewn about with old, but usable sections of cable you happen to need. Or they may have known for months that the lodgepole pine forest across the meadow will be clear-cut next spring . . .

This unfinished fairy-tale cabin sports an unusual roof support design.

6

The Design

The log cabin is a product of the woods and forest. A log cabin should appear to have grown out of the soil on which it stands. It belongs in the country and preferably near a woods. This type of structure would be absolutely out of place in the city surrounded by modern, up-to-date houses or on a skimpy, poorly selected piece of land. Properly constructed and located, the beauty of the log cabin is unique.
—BEN HUNT

How shall your cabin look? What steps lead from a vague impulse well in the back of your mind to a trim cabin set along the edge of the trees in the mountains? It is through the process of design that the thought is transformed into substance. Each cabin-builder can and should perform an individual ritual of design, for your cabin will be a public pronouncement, an extension of yourself. I would sooner suggest what clothes you wear, food you eat, and gods you heed than lay out an array of cabin designs for you to choose from. By slavishly following another's design, you merely rob yourself of the rare experience of being your own architect. The log cabin, in its great generosity, allows you to be your own designer as do few other structures.

The design process is lengthy and involved. You may have dreamed for ten or more years about your cabin before acting upon your dream. Attractive and sound ideas will surge into your mind, and months later will have disappeared. Scores of ideas will have suffered this fate. Suddenly, you have the land, you have with great effort determined to take the time, and you need all those ideas. You will retrieve some, but many are forever lost. At this anxious moment, you face the greatest temptation to gather up all the cabin designs you can find, pick one that suits you, and build, to the nearest inch, what someone else has created. I would like to help you avoid this by offering three general rules of thumb by which to site, design, and construct your cabin. I hope they will prevent some mistakes and yet offer you plenty of creating space. We'll assume that you already have your land.

Site your cabin in accordance with its surroundings. This consideration seems childishly basic, yet it is fre-

quently and disastrously violated. If you have not sketched out your general floor plan, visit your site before you do. If you have sketched it out, take your plan with you, and be prepared to make some alterations, if necessary. Plan for at least a full day at your land. Spend the night there if you can. The job now facing you is that of finding a point of balance, of equilibrium, amidst a multitude of variable factors. Some of these factors are in direct opposition to one another, and with these you cannot have it both ways, and must choose one or the other. You will have an instinctive notion of the best site, but you must look carefully at all factors, with an ever-open mind.

It is necessary to make the following observations and answer the following questions, as well as many others which will be unique to your land. No one but you can provide the required information.

First, find a comfortable place with a good view and sit down. Look carefully about you. Locate the creek or spring. Look at the grass and shrubs around you. Their location and relative thickness will tell you where there may be water, or where there are deep snowdrifts which last late into spring. Can you see any evidence of flooding? Is it quiet? Which way is the wind blowing? Are the trees healthy? If the needles are sparse or yellowing, the trees may be dead within a few years. Where are the new seedlings taking sprout? If there are none, why not? Are you sitting in sun or shade? Any evidence of wildlife activity? How far is it to the road? How does it *feel*, sitting on that particular spot?

Now move to a few other spots and continue to attend closely to what is around you.

One of your most important considerations is your

location with respect to the sun. You are probably in the mountains, so study that North-facing hillside carefully. Will it completely block the sun during those short winter months? Will the sun disappear behind that ridge to the West by three o'clock on summer afternoons? If so, can you escape the ridge's shadow? Mountain-dwellers seek to maximize the direct exposure they receive from the sun, for shade means chill in winter, and late snowdrifts in spring.

Now you have found the best site for sun. What about view? Can you see your neighbors? Where will other cabins be built? Does that matter to you? What sort of view do you really want? Suppose in one direction you have a magnificent vista of dramatic crags but with a gravel pit or road in the foreground, and in another direction, a view of a meadow in the trees, in which you have found signs of elk. Which will be more important to you? Decide and consider more factors.

Where is the water? Can you gravity-feed a water system? If you carry your water, will it be a long haul from the creek? Can you hear the creek splash in its bed? How will you get rid of water and wastes? Is there room for a drainfield? Outhouse? Are these far enough from the water to prevent contamination?

More factors to consider: Is there room for a garden (if the climate allows)? Will it receive enough sun? Can it be watered without great effort or expense? What is the soil like? If a forest fire should occur, can you protect your cabin? Can you get your logs to your site? Can you hear cars on the road? Does the traffic pick up drastically during hunting season? What is the slope of the ground?

The questions seem endless, the possibilities bewildering. You won't be able to think of everything. But you will be able to consider the major factors, and when you trade off one consideration for another, give up another, and perhaps include yet another factor you hadn't foreseen, you will finally decide upon the cabin site.

Again, on the newly-selected site, you must sit down, this time to put your mind's eye to work, for you must now decide on the actual orientation of the cabin on the ground, and on the placement of rooms. Here, too, the sun merits first consideration. Where does it come up and go down? Do you want the sun to rise into the bedroom window or the kitchen window? Can you design your rooms so that it does both? Will the hot afternoon sun make the living room too uncomfortable? From what room will you want to watch the sunsets? Build the woodshed in your imagination. How far will it be from the kitchen? In winter, will you track snow through the living room while carrying the wood to the kitchen? What are the prevailing winds? (This will indicate where your chimney should go and where the snow will pile up.)

The grass, trees, sun, wind, water, and soil are all trying to tell you something: "*Here* is the best place!" or "Right over *there!*" If you listen carefully to them, you will be led unerringly to the best possible site.

You will soon see that you are not nearly as free to decide upon a site as you imagined you were. Such questions will have given your common sense a workout. A framework of restraints is present in the immediate environment of your cabin within which you are free to improvise, but which you are not free to ignore or violate. Careful consideration, you see, lies behind those log cabins which appear to have grown out of the ground on which they stand.

Design your cabin for function, and appearance will take care of itself. As your surroundings impose restraints upon your selection of site, so do your logs impose restraints upon cabin design. In jazz, a performer improvises freely within a prescribed structure of chords and rhythms. A soloist may explore new and exciting melodic lines, but always returns to the original chord structure. In the construction of a log cabin, the logs themselves are the basic harmonic unit. They determine the general appearance of the structure, and will do so, no matter how radical and unorthodox your de-

The builder of this cabin likes odd angles.

sign. Therefore, plan your design on a functional basis. Improvise freely with floor plans, door and window positions, porches, etc. In nearly every instance, the structure will handle the design and still maintain its "log cabin" character.

Your logs are long, slender, heavy, and slightly tapered. That's the way they came out of the woods, and they should be left that way. These characteristics will help you to determine the size of your cabin. You are usually limited by the length of the logs, and by their diameter and weight. If you will be working alone, without machinery, you will not be likely to have fifty-foot logs in your walls. Two persons can easily handle *dry* 35- to 40-foot logs.

A log cabin need not be a one-room structure. A large cabin, say 30' by 30', can easily accommodate a large living room, kitchen, bedroom, bathroom, and loft. The most accurate way to decide upon the cabin size you want is to walk around in somebody else's cabin. You can then quickly decide if you require more or less room, and design accordingly. In general, especially if you will be living in your cabin the year around, think big. Your cabin, like ours, may become your permanent home.

Don't be afraid to improvise. With a few exceptions (see below), you can plan your cabin as you build it. That is, you may plan by stages: floor, walls, roof, built-ins, etc. This provides you with sufficient flexibility to change your mind about some construction details, if you so desire. Let's say that you have decided against building a loft, because you don't feel that you need the space. But once you have the walls up, the cabin feels somewhat smaller than you had imagined and you wish you had planned for a loft. It's not at all too late. You simply add another two or three rounds of logs—to provide for plenty of head room—and build a loft over some portion of the cabin. Or, say you have already cut out the window and door openings and put on the roof. The northeast corner seems a little dark to

you. You may still enlarge the nearest window openings, provided that you make sure that the logs won't shift—an easy job—and solve the light problem.

Variations on your original design will often occur to you as construction proceeds and the three-dimensional character of your cabin begins to materialize. Once your design is set to paper, don't be a slave to it. Let your imagination work for you.

Some details, of course, must be planned before construction begins: number and position of interior walls, fireplace location, some structural members, porches, doors and windows, placement of rooms with respect to function, etc. Even these may be revised at early stages of construction. As you improvise on your original design, it is well to refer back to your plans to see if your proposed alteration will force some other major changes. If, for example, you decide to shift your fireplace foundation a few feet to one side, be sure that its new position doesn't place it directly beneath a planned major roof-supporting member.

In general, the logs enforce a simplicity of design. Your cabin is likely to have compact, rather than sweeping lines, to be broad and have lots of square corners. If your design truly reflects your basic needs, it will reflect its builder. It may not become Taliesen West, or be featured in *Architectural Forum,* but it will please your eye and provide repose.

This unusual log home has no internal support members (columns, trusses, etc.). Two steel cables strung just below the eaves provide the key structural support.

7

Getting Ready

If you are, say, twenty-five, you are not likely to agonize for long over the prospect of moving to the woods and building a cabin. You have few vested interests to abandon, you are flushed with optimism and probably determined not to emulate your elders; you are adventurous by sheer dint of age. Anything is possible.

But if you are, say, thirty-five, your world has different dimensions. You have a steady job, perhaps a family. Career advancement and prestige beckon. You may be a little uneasy about your society, but you don't build bombs. You are reasonably affluent. You have heard of people who have left all their security behind them to find a rich and fulfilling life in the woods, but you've never actually met such a person, so you are vaguely uneasy. It seems to you that you have something to lose.

By far the most critical preparation you must make is inside your head. You are contemplating a shift from a materially secure situation to an uncertain, new, and slightly frightening endeavor. You don't need fanciful illusions, but you do need to set a positive, self-assured frame of mind for yourself. The best way to do this would be to visit people who have made such a move and judge for yourself. But this may not be possible, so the next best thing is to read about such things.

The books that will help you fall into four major categories: survival, adventure, underground, and philosophical. Each category offers a somewhat different approach to the same problem, each will provide you with useful information, and each contains both excellent and poor books, so you will need to read selectively. I will suggest the categories, but you must sift among them to find what is most useful for your unique situation.

Survival. Bookstores are suddenly flooded with sur- vival books. These are books which tell you what to eat, how to keep warm, fashion tools, prepare shelter, navigate, make clothes, etc., etc, if you should suddenly be parachuted naked into the far north woods. You may not be planning on such an event. Neither am I. But a look through a few of these books will provide you with some of the flavor of life in the woods, and give you an idea of the importance of problem-solving in getting along there. As in log cabin building, the skills are ultimately acquired by doing rather than by reading. Your bookstore will probably have about ten titles in this category and the dealer will be happy to direct you to them.

Adventure. This category includes personal experiences, usually narratives by people who have radically changed their life styles by moving to wilderness or semi-wilderness areas, building their homes, raising their families, facing the unknown, etc. The titles are usually something like *Two Against the Wilderness,* or *Life in the North Woods,* or *We Chose the Arctic,* or something similar. Some are rather dull, other are sensitive accounts of real-life adventures. All convey a sense of dramatic renewal of vitality, of dogged perserverance in the face of adversity. The books in this category are, without exception, success stories; those who fail to meet the challenges probably don't write books about it. Many of these books date back to post-World War II, but their message is as appropriate now as it was then. Try your local librarian for these books.

Underground. This category includes the efforts of those young men and women who were the first to sound the ecological alarm. Environmentalists have been around for considerably longer than the underground press, of course, but their voices were generally lonely

Unusual windows can be created with a chain saw and ingenuity.

cries in the wilderness until an outraged generation of young people gave common currency to the phrases "quality of life" and "alternative life style." Those publications which relate to going "back to the land," changing life styles, providing your own shelter, etc., are usually well-illustrated paperbacks. This is an especially rich category, replete with provoking ideas and solid information. There are books on alternative energy sources, organic gardening, living on next-to-nothing, obtaining land cheaply, modern homesteading techniques, where-to-get or how-to-make almost anything, etc., etc. The publications tend to be polemic in style and the authors are emphatic about their own point of view. But they are articulate and express a sense of youthful urgency. There will be a couple of shelves of books in this category at your bookstore, and you'll probably find a half-dozen or so which will relate somehow to your particular aspirations. Most public libraries, not surprisingly, don't mess with them. Hence the appellation, "underground."

Philosophical. This category will serve the heavy intellectuals among you. If you need to bolster or augment the philosophical underpinnings of your proposed move, and the elation so evident in the books in the "adventure" category will not suffice, look into the writings of some men who have lived or extolled the virtues of simple and active lives, close to nature: Ralph Waldo Emerson, John Muir, Scott Nearing, Wendell Berry, Henry David Thoreau. For poetry: Gary Snyder, Walt Whitman. Once again, your librarian.

None of these categories will provide you with an easy answer to the question, "Should I go to the woods?" Neither will the tarot, *I Ching,* or your star chart. Remember that you are seeking tools to help in establishing a healthy, positive mind-set toward your new activity. Such a frame of mind can emerge only from your own experience. But you will find in these books that others have shared bits and pieces of your experience, even your anxieties, and have, in the end,

prevailed. If you have serious doubts about the wisdom of your plans, spend some time with the books. You have nothing to lose, but you may by your efforts be granted the gift of transforming dreams into realities.

One final book category: books on log cabins. It is an important subject that I prefer to cover in detail, and it is discussed in Chapter X. So if you're into buying books right now, look there.

Once you have achieved a log cabin frame of mind, all the other tasks involved in getting ready become much easier. Before long, almost everything you do is directed somehow toward your goal. Let's say, for instance, that the old clunker you drive finally gives out. Normally, one hopes, you would think to yourself, "Well, I'll minimize my personal drain on dwindling fossil fuel supplies and get a VW bug." But now that you are log cabin minded, you think ahead and realize that you will need to scrounge mountains of materials and move them to your site. You will probably need to negotiate a rough road, at times through mud or snow. You may need to drag logs. You therefore buy a sturdy and large pickup instead of a VW bug. You will be appalled at your gas mileage, and your ecological conscience will plague you every time you pull into a gas station. The trade-off is nevertheless positive, for in the long run your wilderness home will tax orthodox energy systems far less than a city home. Your pickup has become your first tangible commitment to a new way of life.

You have been saving money, always a hard task, and putting it into an inviolable land fund. You go without rather than touch that fund. And all this time you have been looking for the land.

Searching for land can be a time-consuming, frustrating drag, which cannot be avoided. The price of land in remote areas is creeping steadily upwards, as ever-increasing numbers of people seek it. The only way to acquire a sense of what you need is to search and compare, search and compare. You will have to haunt realtors' offices, faithfully review the classified section, search out unorthodox sources, and drive mile after mile, looking and looking. After several fruitless months of searching, I finally obtained exactly what I needed only through sheer luck. I would not depend upon luck as the solution to the problem, however. Again, some books may help. A few people have compiled and published some techniques which will help you with your land-search. I have included their titles in Chapter X.

An important preparatory task is acquiring the tools you will need to build your cabin. Chapter IX is devoted to the tools themselves. You should learn what tools you will need and begin to gather them as early as possible, since proper tools for log construction are becoming increasingly difficult to obtain.

Start keeping a sharp eye out for tools at garage sales and auctions. A word on auctions—you can stretch your dollars considerably by purchasing tools and building materials at auctions, but you can also get burned, so here are a few suggestions to help you get started.

Go to one or two auctions before you actively buy, to learn the rules followed in your locale and to get the feel of the auctioneers. Always arrive before the sale begins, so that you can check over the merchandise. Stay away from auctions in resort areas, for summer residents will drive up the prices. Avoid auctions which are widely and garishly advertised. If possible, bid at the beginning or at the end of the sale. At the start of an auction the auctioneer needs to feel out the crowd and often lets the first several items go very cheaply in order to stimulate the bidding; when the crowd has thinned out toward the end of the sale, the auctioneer will often accept exceptionally low bids for a whole pile of goods. As for bidding, set yourself an upper limit on an item, and stick to it. There will always be more auctions, and more bargains.

If you are to build your cabin cheaply, you must also begin to gather building materials early—well before you begin construction. To obtain tools and building materials at low or no cost, you must elevate scrounging to the level of a finely disciplined art, becoming a consumate gatherer of resources. Skillful scrounging requires a balanced blend of cheeky gall and velvet-gloved diplomacy, sharp eyes and ears, lots of smiles, a keenly-honed vigilance for potentially required materials, patience, and damned hard work. Never buy what you might get free if you ask for it in the right way. Never buy that for which you can trade your labor. You will blow it sometimes. I somehow accumulated (and paid for) several boxes of bolts which apparently fit nothing but turn-of-the-century locomotives. But I also unknowingly acquired countless odd items which I was able to put to excellent use in construction later on.

What building materials—apart from logs—will you need to accumulate? At first thought, it seems like you require an endless supply of nearly everything, and there will be days on the job when it seems as though you've run out of everything at once. But after your original panic subsides, and you cast the cold clear light of reason on your supply problem, you will realize that there are five basic supplies you will need in appreciable quantities. They are lumber, stone materials (bricks, sand and gravel, rocks), spikes and nails, chinking and caulking materials, and paints and sealers. Concentrate your scrounging efforts on these materials and you will find that you pick up the other things you need along the way.

It is impossible to put these materials into some logical and precise order of acquisition. Your needs will vary in accordance with your cabin design, location, local resources, and plain luck.

Perhaps the highest priority should be assigned to lumber, simply because you will need lots of it. My wife and I utilized every scrap of lumber we accumulated and always seemed to require more. You will need some lumber even before you begin construction of the cabin itself—for stakes, foundation batter boards, to build ladders and mitre boxes, perhaps a bridge across a creek to your site, etc. Turn down very little at this stage of preparation if it is cheap enough. Anything from railroad ties to lath is likely to find use. You can get selective later, when you know what sizes you need for a particular stage of construction.

How do you know if the lumber is cheap enough? In order to determine this, you must be able to glance at a stack of lumber and quickly convert it to approximate board feet. This means spending time at lumber yards, getting market prices and learning to think about lumber in terms of board feet. You can't avoid spending some time with paper and pencil. At auctions you won't always have time for careful measurements, so learn to estimate quantities quickly, and keep abreast of lumber yard prices, for they fluctuate wildly. Put a tape measure in your pocket, and leave it there. It will come in handy for lumber measurements and you will soon depend on it for other measurements.

The best bargain, of course, is free lumber. If your scrounging skills are highly developed, you may find people who will *pay* you to take down a building containing materials you need. More likely, you will be given salvage privileges in exchange for removing a building. To take a building down carefully requires nearly as much care and effort as it took to put it up. You will need a few special tools (See Chapter IX). If you wear tennis shoes on this job you will be getting nail punctures and tetanus shots. It might be a good idea to get a tetanus antitoxin shot anyway. Work carefully, for old lumber splits easily. Keep a weather eye out for long pieces, especially those which are well-matched in width and length. Sort the lumber carefully, with special attention to thickness. Older sawmills often cut timber according to requested specifications, rather than to modern standard sizes. After the building is down and your lumber sorted, maintain your good reputation by thoroughly cleaning up the site.

Obtaining lumber by taking down old buildings will

cost you considerably more time and effort than going to the lumber yard, it is true. The returns for your effort take the form of saving hard-earned cash, meeting some of your neighbors, and obtaining lumber which will not shrink. All lumber, of course, "breathes." That is, it shrinks and swells, especially across the grain, according to time of day, time of year, or prevailing weather conditions. But old lumber has thoroughly dried, and "breathes" within tolerable limits. The so-called kiln-dried lumber you buy can shrink as much as 15% of its width—*after* you have carefully fitted and nailed it into place. Scrounging for old lumber is therefore not simply a means to save a few bucks, but an exercise in obtaining quality building materials. The savings, however, can be considerable. In order to provide dimension lumber for my own cabin—a large one—I took down three buildings. Two were free. One was bought at an auction. Total investment: $15, some gasoline, and two days' work.

Stone materials include the sand, gravel, rocks, bricks, cement, and lime you will need for the foundation, fireplace, porch, perhaps walkways. Most of these materials are free or cheap. You may be lucky enough to have plenty of clean sand, gravel, and rocks close at hand. Most people are not. Look over your local supply carefully, for much of that stone lying around may not be suitable for use where it would be exposed to view. But by all means use as much immediately local stone as you can. We were fortunate enough to have fossil-bearing strata around us, and were thus able to adorn our porch with rocks containing clam-like brachiopods, delicate corals, and the whorled shells of fossil ammonites, and yet leave plenty of fossils behind for others to discover.

You will probably have to buy cement and lime, but try to scrounge bricks. Used brick is not only much cheaper than new brick, but also more pleasing to the eye. You will have to accumulate lots of heavy stone material. Now you begin to appreciate your pickup.

Nails and spikes can be very expensive, so keep a sharp lookout for these items at auctions, garage sales, etc. You will eventually find use for most sizes, but look especially for 16-penny or so common nails (for securing two-inch lumber), roofing nails (for nailing down rolled roofing), and spikes (ten inches or so long, for spiking down logs). Use galvanized nails in places that are likely to get wet. They'll hold better and won't streak your logs and window frames with rust stains. Don't buy special use fasteners (such as hardened cement nails, expansion nails, brads, staples, etc.) in large quantities, but rather only as you need them. They're expensive, and you might find that you don't need them after all.

Depending on your location, pocketbook and taste, your chinking and caulking materials might be oakum, fibreglass insulation, quarter rounds, red clay, mortar, or sphagnum moss. Essentially, chinking materials fill in the big holes between the logs, and caulking compounds then go over the top of the chinking or to fill in the little holes or seams. The relative merits of each of these materials is discussed in Chapter XVI. It will be necessary to stockpile some sort of chinking and caulking materials, so decide which suits you best at an early date. Don't put it off for too long.

Paints and sealers, as used here, is a catch-all term for the various solutions you will be applying to both inside and outside wood surfaces to protect and preserve them. More details on these later.

There are, of course, other supplies to gather: glass, screws, stovepipe, window and door hardware, flooring and roofing material, wire, pipe and plumbing fixtures, etc. But if you concentrate on the five classes of building materials discussed above, you will accumulate at an early stage the most critical supplies, and should not be forced to halt construction for lack of materials.

Before considering logs, let's discuss doors and windows. I recommend 1) that you build them yourself rather than buy or scrounge them, and 2) that you have them built and framed well before you begin to lay your foundation or start notching logs.

As you thumb through your log cabin books and pause at the diagrams for window and door construction, you are likely to experience some nervous discomfort, for the diagrams are rather complicated, and labeled with strange new words like spline, casement, mortise and tenon, chamfer, screen rebate, etc., etc. Obviously, those words mean something important, but you aren't quite sure what, so you think to yourself, 'I probably wouldn't be able to build the damned things anyway.' At this point, you go to your local lumber yard to buy some simple pre-framed windows. There, the salesman convinces you that aluminum-framed windows with built-in screens are better, and so all because of a twinge of discomfort you wind up with very expensive windows that look awful in your cabin.

You can avoid this hassle and expense either by scrounging used windows or by building your own. Many old windows are more attractive than the modern mass-produced models. But they often have to be reputtied throughout—a slow, tedious job—and because you must take what you find, you have little control over the size and style of windows you will use. If, however, you build your own, you may make your own determination of size and style. If you decide that you must have windows which swing or slide up and down, and are festooned with all manner of fancy trim, then you *will* need to know what all those strange words mean, and the carpentry techniques and concepts which go along with them.

There is another way . . .

If you build windows which *do not open,* there is no need for the fanciwork. Such windows are little more than a frame, some molding, a piece of glass, some glazing compound, and a few nails. Such windows can be built quickly, and if you scrounge the lumber and glass, cheaply. "Absurd," you say, "imagine windows which don't open. How does one get a breeze?"

Above, left: This window does not open. The screened ventilator below it provides air circulation. From this window, the builder once watched a mountain lion, one of the neighbors with whom he shares this mountain valley. Above, right: A different window design with the ventilator above the window.

The answer is in a book by Rex Roberts, entitled *Your Engineered House*. This is an excellent book, loaded with lots of revolutionary ideas about houses that will help you with your own design. Regarding windows, Roberts argues that the inherent functions of windows are to control the amount of light which enters a house and to allow the inhabitants to see out effectively. It is when we try to make windows control light *and* heat *and* ventilation that problems arise. For instance, if your house is too hot, you open the window (usually two or more) to provide a cross-breeze to cool it off. Then, because there are bugs in the great out-of-doors, you put screens on your windows. Most screens reduce the passage of light by 30%. So in order to cool your house, you have had to appreciably diminish your effective view and have had to darken your house by nearly one-third! And if your windows are not cleverly placed with respect to the compass points, there will be days when you will not get any breeze anyway. Roberts suggests

Right, top: "Barn sash" windows are particularly appealing in log homes. Fiberglass insulation is loosely stuffed between logs before quarter-round chinking is nailed into place. Right, center: The tall, narrow windows illustrated here can be exceptionally appealing in log walls. Right, bottom: Vertical corner posts allow window installation close to corners.

avoiding this and other problems by using windows for light control only, and by controlling heat and ventilation through the use of ventilators built into the window frames. The location of the ventilators is important, since the ventilation system is based upon convection principles. The system takes advantage of the fact that warm air rises, to be replaced by cool air. If you can effect control over this event, you can provide yourself with a breeze. To do so, you position ventilators high on one side of the house and low on the other side. Thus, when you open them, convection takes over, and presto, a breeze. For maximum efficiency, the high ventilators should be placed on the warmer side of the structure, usually the South- and West-facing sides, and the lower ventilators on the cooler North and East sides. Refer to Roberts' book for more theory and details.

Roberts puts his system to work in frame houses, but his arguments were so sensible that my wife and I suppressed our own doubts (who, after all, ever heard of a house with windows that don't open?), built the windows and ventilators as units, and installed them in our own log cabin. They are a resounding success. They were easy to build and inexpensive. We can control the breeze easily and quickly, no bugs get in, and we don't have to bother with screens for the windows. Since they don't open, they don't jam up or rattle, and with the vents open, we hear the coyotes, crickets, and curlews. (See illustrations)

The advantages of building your windows, of whatever style, ahead of time are speed (in town you can use power tools, go to the glass shop, get screen and mold-

Left, below: An upright corner support allows windows to be installed in corners which may otherwise be relatively dark. Note that the wall logs were grooved by hand rather than with a chain saw.

ing, etc.) and the delightful fact that when you have the walls of your cabin up and the roof on, you merely cut out the window holes, spike in vertical braces at the sides, slip in the window frame, nail it into place, and you are done. You can add trim later, but you have window units in place which will provide you with plenty of light, as much breeze as you want, and which will keep the mosquitoes in their natural habitat—outside. (See illustrations)

Exterior doors present a different problem. Most store-bought doors simply do not grace a log cabin. They are usually light and thin, whereas a well-built cabin conveys a sense of weight and density. A proper log cabin door should insulate, provide protection from gnawing rodents and foraging bears, and from vandals. It should contribute to the sturdy appearance of the cabin. You will have trouble finding commercial doors you can afford which fulfill these functions, so at least consider the possibility of building your own doors—well ahead of time, like your windows. Handsome doors are expensive to buy, but relatively inexpensive to build.

Getting ready to start building your cabin can be one of the most important and most pleasant stages of your new activity. The anticipation is breathtaking. You are psychologically committed to the cabin, buoyant and full of confidence. You've finally found your land—at a reasonable price, it is hoped—and you are busy gathering together building materials and tools. There is one other major item to consider, and we'll take up that subject next—the logs themselves.

Left, above: It is nearly impossible to buy a commercially-built door which graces a hand-built log home. Hence, log builders almost invariably build their own. This one is a handsome example with hardware that complements the solidity of the cabin itself. **Left, below:** Careful window preparation. Note the short section of 2 x 4 inserted into the spline cut into the inside edge of the window opening. The 2 x 4 will keep the logs in proper vertical alignment while allowing them to settle unimpeded. The use of milled three-sided logs is popular in Fairbanks, Alaska, where this cabin is located.

Above, left: Note the use of quarter-logs for door framing. Center: Three-inch timbers and strap iron make for a beautiful, durable door. Right: A well-designed basement door. The cement block foundation will eventually be faced with fieldstone.

Below, left: A door constructed with and held together by half-poles. Center: Notice the quarter-pole door frame and the glass panels in this door. Right: An artistic glass design renders these doors unique.

8

Logs

What kind of logs should you use?

Virtually all of the recently built cabins in Western America are constructed with evergreen logs, from the cone-bearing, needle-leafed trees (pine, fir, spruce, larch, etc.). If you browse through the cabin books, you will find that certain species of trees are recommended as superior to others for construction purposes. Cedar is usually considered the most desirable building log, for it is long and straight, and its resins render it decay-resistant. Unfortunately, the same qualities make for excellent telephone poles, so the trees are much in demand and expensive. Larch (tamarack) has many favorable building qualities, but it is very hard when dry and is considered by some to be least desirable. There is little agreement among cabin builders on the relative values of various species, and in practice, they usually wind up using the best evergreen logs available to them, whatever the species. So let's first consider what constitutes a good log.

The ideal building log is straight, with little or no taper. It has few knots or bumps. It is not twisted, bowed, or corkscrewed in shape. Insects have not bored into it, nor has fungus discolored it. Neither too soft nor too hard, it does not have a "swell-butt," nor a "cat-face" from bark abrasion, nor lightning scars. Its bark peels smoothly and easily from the sapwood. It is located a mere two hundred feet from your cabin site, and it has dozens of neighbors just like it.

Let's face it, there are no such logs . . . at least not very many of them. Get yourself as many logs as you can which approach our ideal log, and do your best with the rest. The logs in an even-aged stand of timber may look monotonously uniform to you, but once they are cut, peeled, and stacked, their uneven and irregular character is striking. Even your most careful and patient selection of trees will result in some flawed logs. That's

all right, though, because you will usually be able to correct the problems the odd ones will cause.

Here are some general rules for selection of logs:

For construction purposes, diameter is more important than length. Try to select logs of similar thickness, rather than logs of different diameters, but with similar lengths. It is difficult, though not impossible, to work with logs which differ more than, say, two to three inches in diameter. It takes lots of looking to carefully match logs for diameter. Nature abhors monotony, as well as vacuums, so when you use natural building materials as is, you must accept their basic irregularity. If you must have precise uniformity, you can use milled logs, but you will trade off both cash and appearance for that machined regularity. So keep looking around and you'll eventually find logs that match in diameter closely enough for your purposes.

Select only logs with very little taper. This means more looking, but I assure you that the time is well spent now rather than later. Logs with extreme taper can cause you serious headaches and lots of extra work later. Let us say that you are ambitious, and your design calls for forty-foot logs on one wall. You will probably find that there are plenty of trees around which will supply a forty-foot log 15 inches at the butt and 9 inches at the tip, but only one in ten will taper from, say 14 inches to 12 inches in forty feet. It is a great temptation to cut those abundant, tapered trees and get busy building. Resist the temptation, for at the corners of your cabin the butt of one log intersects the tip of another, and you may find yourself trying to join together smoothly logs which are nearly twice as big as one another. Visualize notching a large log to receive a small one and you'll grasp the problem. Worse, the problem compounds as successive "rounds" of logs are laid down.

The effective length of your logs is determined by

This builder provided a strongly supported eave which is an integral part of the house design by two techniques: he allowed the ends of the eighth wall log and joist logs to extend several feet beyond the corner, and he installed a purlin between each gable log.

their taper. A fifty-five foot log with a sharp taper is not a fifty-five foot building log, for the reasons described above. Its useful length to you may only be thirty feet. Keep effective length in mind as you design your cabin and as you become familiar with the characteristics of the local trees. You may find that the forests in your area simply do not produce many tall, straight trees, and you may have to work that long continuous wall out of your design. Or the gods may smile, and you will discover a single stand of trees which has been provided with just the right amount of sunlight, shelter, and moisture to produce precisely the long logs that you require.

If you have selected your logs with regard to uniform diameter, minimal taper, and effective length, you will have no serious log-related problems during construction. But if you are like most cabin-builders, you have logs which are odd-sized in nearly every respect, and you go ahead and build your cabin anyway. *C'est la vie*.

Some minor points:

Look in even-aged stands of trees for your cabin logs. The stands are easy to recognize. The trees are all about the same size and height—which is why you're there looking. Usually a fire or logging operation disrupted the original forest, so that the new trees all took root at about the same time. Avoid trees from hilltops, steep slopes, or at the edges of stands. Such trees are exposed to strong winds and severe extremes of temperature, and are frequently bowed or have sharply twisted grain which is hidden by the bark. A dense, but not thick stand of trees in a sheltered, fairly level spot will be the most promising place to look.

If possible, avoid trees with lots of low branches. Most evergreens prune themselves as they grow. When their lower branches become shaded and thus less efficient producers of food for the tree, they are simply dropped off. Some trees, notably spruce and douglas fir, are less efficient self-pruners and have lots of low branches which you must cut. These branches slow up several jobs: peeling, notching, flattening, drilling. The knots are also hard on bladed tools. You will always have some knots to contend with. Fine, for they are attractive on the peeled log. Just try to keep the number of them down to something reasonable.

What size should your logs be?

This depends, of course, on the size of your cabin. As a rule of thumb, figure about 8 inches as a minimum, about 14 as a maximum. Logs smaller than 8 inches will require you to spend too much time chinking and caulking. It takes lots of 6-inch logs to make a ten-foot high wall, and it means lots of notches to chop out. Logs bigger than about 14 inches, on the other hand, are difficult to handle, particularly if you're working alone. These precautions *do not* mean that you shouldn't even attempt to work with larger or smaller logs, but rather that there are special factors to consider, like plenty of time to work with small logs, and some hard thinking about levers, pulleys, and cables when working with extra large logs. The main point to remember is to get even-sized logs. Sure, you'll find use for the odd large and small ones, but most of them should be about the same size.

How many logs with you need?

This will depend upon your cabin's size, number of interior log walls, and the diameter of your logs. For a small cabin, say 20′ by 20′, 40 to 60 logs; for a 30′ by 30′ cabin, 80 to 120 logs. Always get a few more than you think you will need, for you will cull out some logs for various reasons. If you are able to obtain longer logs than you had anticipated, with even, gentle taper, go back to your design and lengthen a wall or two. Stay flexible. Remember, though, to allow four to six feet of extra length if you want your logs to project beyond the corners in the classic log cabin style. And if you are planning on long roof overhangs for eaves or porches, allow for even more extra length. (See illustrations)

Remember to allow purlins, rafters, and second story floor beams to extend well beyond the walls in order to provide support for structure such as this porch.

You will also need poles. Floor and ceiling joists, rafter, railings, and various trim features can be constructed with poles. For the most appealing appearance, use poles for visible structural supports, such as rafters, and dimension lumber for hidden supports, such as floor joists. (See illustrations) The latter present you with the classic trade-off decision. If you have enough cash, you can buy dimension lumber and install the joists without too much effort. *Or* you can have them nearly free if you use poles and are willing to peel them, square their ends, and hew a flat spot along their entire length.

Should you season your logs?

A tough decision, this one. There are two schools of thought. The dry log school advises you to select and cut your logs six months to a year before you begin to build your cabin. The advantages: such logs will have dried and shrunk; they will not shrink appreciably after they are put up; they are much lighter in weight than green logs, and thus easier to handle. The objections: very few people have the luxury of time required to season logs for several months, most builders decide fast and move fast; the logs may discolor while seasoning unattended; dry logs are hard logs, so your bladed tools will require appreciably more maintenance; finally, they might get ripped off while they are stacked there, drying.

The green log school advises you to select your logs, fall them, peel them, and put them up. The advantages: foremost, of course, is being able to use them right away; if you should run short, you just go out and get another, and don't worry about letting it season for several months; green logs are softer and may be "worked" more easily than dry logs; discoloration can be controlled as construction proceeds. The objections: green logs will shrink (in diameter—only negligibly in length), requiring that allowance be made for subsequent settling at door and window openings; they are much heavier and harder to handle than dry logs.

Follow the advice of either school. If you have time, season the logs. If you don't have time or opportunity, use green logs, and don't worry about it. In either case, your cabin will be durable and beautiful, a joy to your heart.

A final word on logs: if you are a perfectionist, an impulsive specialist, always in a hurry and impatient with your own mistakes, prepare to change your ways or read no further. Log cabins may not be for you. One takes up the task of building a log cabin with patience, methodical work, and love. You will make mistakes, false starts . . . and then correct them, a wiser builder. The materials themselves are imperfect. You will need to take your time and think out each new step, and you will need patience to slowly learn each of the skills you will eventually acquire.

Patience, a methodical approach, love . . . and tools, which we discuss next.

This cabin will have a step-down living room. The foundation posts are treated cedar. Closely spaced, heavy floor joists (right) will provide a strong and solid floor. Note the strips of fiberglass insulation laid between successive rounds of wall logs in the background.

9

Hand Tools

Believe one who knows: you will find
something greater in woods than in books.
Trees and stones will teach you that which you
can never learn from masters.
—ST. BERNARD DE CLAIRVAUX

Jobs done well with proper tools are the source of many of your most satisfying experiences while building your cabin. Jobs you screw up for lack of a proper tool provide you with excruciating frustration and may provoke enraged outbursts at the sky, your dog, and your innocent wife. You can spare yourself—and your loved ones—much of this abuse if you will calmly begin to collect tools you will need well ahead of time.

I have compiled in this chapter the tools I found necessary to build my own cabin. It is not a comprehensive list. Sometimes neighbors or friends loaned me some tool or other; sometimes I made one tool do several different sorts of jobs, including some for which it was not really intended. The latter is poor practice, for it is hard on the nerves and hard on the tools. You may not need all of the tools listed in this chapter. I did.

If you hurry out and buy all of these tools new, you and several hundred dollars will soon be parted. There are better uses for that money, like making land payments. So take your time, keep your cool, and buy most of your tools secondhand. You will be amazed at the difference in price between, say, a new and used hammer. Yet either one will drive nails properly.

The best sources of used tools are garage sales, rummage sales, farm, ranch, or estate auctions, or from the want ads in your local newspaper. Sometimes secondhand stores will provide tool bargains, but it is preferable to get your tools at the same places that the secondhand dealers get theirs. Avoid antique dealers assiduously, for here you will be asked to pay inflated prices for archaic tools valued as quaint objects of curiosity, rather than as working equipment. It matters little that you need them to do your work. Try to find a cheap broadaxe and you will see what I mean.

The first group of tools include those which will be used in your preliminary lumber-scrounging activities, as well as in the cabin construction:

Nail-puller, known by experienced scroungers as the thumb-smasher. This ingenious and treacherous gadget will help you remove lumber from old buildings without splitting or breaking it.

Crowbar. Used for the same thing.

Hammers. You need a sixteen-ounce claw hammer and, for driving spikes later on, a five-pound blacksmith hammer or sledge.

Shovels. Get two. One regular round-point and one square-ended cement shovel.

For the cabin construction:

Chain saw. By now you will have decided whether or not to use this tool on your logs. If you have decided against it, skip the following paragraph.

This is one tool that you should consider buying new, unless you are pretty handy with small engines. Like many machines, it ensnares you by making you dependent upon it. So consider yourself snared, and get a saw you can depend upon to start when you pull the cord. Do not get a large chain saw. A light saw with a fourteen-inch bar will suffice. It is important that it be light, so it won't throw you off balance when you are astraddle a log twenty feet above the ground, and small in order to perform rather fine work. At times you may have to hold it with one hand. Learn how to sharpen the damned thing and keep it that way, or it will begin to saw gentle curves before you notice it. Some of its uses: falling and bucking your logs and poles, sawing out window and doorholes, making tight fits between adjacent logs, cutting rough lumber for various purposes, starting round notches, cutting up firewood, etc. A chain saw cuts well

A "Norwegian log scribe," used in chinkless-style log work.

across the grain. It will not rip (saw parallel to the grain) very efficiently.

Axe. The most important tool. There are some jobs that only your axe will do. It will also, if necessary, do many jobs for which you would ordinarily use another tool. It is probably the most versatile of your growing collection of tools, and you'll be very well acquainted with its many capabilities soon after you begin to lay logs. I recommend a small (26-28 inch) double-bitted cruising axe (See illustration). It should be short, since you will need to use it in tight places, and you will frequently have to "choke" the handle, as one chokes a

baseball bat. A longer, heavier axe is a more suitable tool for falling your logs, if you should decide to forego a chain saw. But you are going to have to develop no small measure of skill with the smaller axe in order to notch your logs later, so you might as well begin to get the feel of it right away. You should have two of these axes, of identical length and weight. A spare axe will enable you to continue work while the other is out of commission. This is important because at certain stages of construction nearly all labor is axe-work, and replacing a loose or broken axe handle is a time-consuming job. This most important tool is also the most dangerous

The tools of the trade. Tools leaning against log (l. to r.): froe, peeling spuds or slicks (2), nail-puller, axe, cant hook. Foreground (l. to r.): log dogs (3), punch, augers (2). Far right: lug hook. Note scribe stuck in log at upper right.

HAND TOOLS   55

if mishandled, and is deadliest when it is dull. Keep it sharp. Check the head frequently for looseness, and the handle for cracks. Learn how to sharpen it safely, how to replace a weakened handle, and keep a small supply of wedges on hand to keep the axe-head tight. You should not use your carefully sharpened notching axe for cutting firewood, clearing brush, etc.

Hatchet. There will be a few jobs that require axe work, but for which you will not be able to use the axe. A constricted corner, an awkward angle, or a position too precarious to allow a two-handed swing may rule out use of your axe. In these instances, a hatchet, and nothing else, will usually perform the work. It is just as dangerous as an axe, and needs to be maintained as carefully.

Files. These are maintenance tools. You need flat files for sharpening your bladed tools, round files for keeping the saw chain sharp.

Draw knife. (See illustration.) You will spend many hours with this tool. Only a peeling spud will strip the bark from your logs as neatly or as quickly. Only the axe will raise more blisters than the draw knife. The blade need not be wider than eight inches, since most of your logs will have small diameters. These tools are hard to find, but you'll bark fewer knuckles and be able to reach tighter spots if you can find one with folding handles. Try very hard to get *two* draw knives.

Peeling spud or *slick* (See illustration.) This long-handled tool is also used for peeling bark from logs. It has a sturdy blade about three inches wide. You will have to have one made, or make it yourself. Although some builders consider it to be a better tool than the draw knife for peeling logs, the peeling spud is not as versatile as the draw knife. It works very well on green logs.

Log dogs (See illustration.) If you ask your local hardware dealer for "log dogs," you are likely to be sent to a pet store, because he will not know what they are. These devices are used to "dog" logs into place while you work on them (that is, to fix them firmly in a desired, usually temporary, position). You are not apt to be able to find them ready-made, but they are simple tools which you can have made cheaply. They should be made of heavy metal rod (about 5/8 inch diameter) since they will be hammered repeatedly into logs. The pointed sections should be about four inches long and the overall length no less than 24 inches; 36 inches is about right. If they are shorter, they will constantly be in your way when you are hewing out notches. Those log dogs which have chisel-like points set at right angles to each other are not recommended. They are hard to pound in and chew up your logs. You will need about six dogs.

Scribe. This is the tool with which you mark the exact size and position of the notches to be made, and with which you determine how much of a log to trim for a close fit to an adjacent log. The "Norwegian" scribe (see illustration) is used primarily in "chinkless" log work to obtain an accurate fit between logs. It will not usually open widely enough to scribe for the notches. For marking notches, scribes which will adjust to widths of several inches are required. (See illustrations.) You will probably have to build or improvise your own scribe. Spend some money on this tool. Obtain or make a scribe equipped with a level; one which can be adjusted firmly in any position. Get one to which a soft-lead pencil or felt-tipped pen can be attached. You will need to interchange them. Some pens (and sometimes pencils) will not mark damp logs clearly. A faulty or inadequate scribe or careless scribing will often cause faulty notching, which will cause you endless trouble, befuddlement, and frustration. The most skilled axemen cannot make a poorly scribed notch fit well without repeated trial and error, and a serious error may cost you the use of a carefully selected log.

Adze and broadaxe. These tools are recommended by many who write about log construction. They are used primarily for flattening a portion or the entire length of logs. The only ones we found available were in antique stores, at prohibitive prices. We then found that

Left: Tools: foreground, adjustable scribe with line level taped to top; upper left, two drawknives; right, wood chisel and lignum vitae mallet. Right: Scribe—the tool which enables the builder to hew tightly fitting notches such as the one illustrated. A small line level is firmly taped to the right hand leg of the scribe to ensure that the two points are perpendicular to each other while scribing. Punch in foreground.

the axe, hatchet or chain saw would do the required work, without any apparent cost in time, effort, or workmanship. In my opinion, they are not essential tools for this type of work, although they would certainly be useful for certain jobs.

Chisels. (Again, see the illustration.) You will need at least two chisels—one for rough and one for fine work. Several sizes are useful, but these tools are expensive. I recommend a 1¾-inch chisel for rough work and a ¾-inch chisel for finer shaping. These sizes will also enable you to notch channels for two-inch and one-inch dimension lumber. A curved gouge chisel with an outside bevel is frequently recommended for close-fitting, "cupped" notches. This is an expensive, hard-to-find tool. We found that a sharp, carefully wielded axe would do a good job.

Hand drills and bits, and augers. A brace and several drill bits will be useful. Procure one bit which will drill one-inch holes. (You'll be driving spikes in these holes later.) Another useful though expensive bit is called a "bell hanger." It is about 18 inches long and will drill a clean hole through the middle of your largest

logs. A hand-powered rotary drill is useful for finish work. Augers (see illustration) are part of the classic tool collection for log work. They, too, are difficult to find and museum-priced when they are available. I found a two-inch auger at an auction, but found few uses for it.

Tape measures. You need a fifty-foot steel tape and an eight- or sixteen-foot pocket tape. Even if your cabin is only thirty by thirty, you'll still need that fifty-foot tape. Get tapes that won't stretch.

Level. Begin by trusting your eye. For most purposes, your eyeball judgement will be close enough. If possible, get somebody else to eyeball it, too. There will be instances in which your eye will instruct you to place a log or board in some position which is not perfectly horizontal or vertical, but is simply correct or pleasing.

But . . . there are instances in which a precisely level or perpendicular placement is of critical importance. Windows, doors, floor joists, fireplace or stove foundation, etc. For these jobs, use a level, or risk crooked windows, wavy floors, or finding all the bacon grease in the downhill side of your frying pan. A thirty-six inch level will do nicely, if you also carefully pick out a very straight, long, and dry 2 x 4 to use to level over longer spans.

Carpenter's Square. If your eye is sharp enough to cut straight lines and determine square corners, consider yourself very fortunate indeed. My eye is not so sharp, so I depend upon a battered carpenter's square. I should point out now that not one in a hundred visitors to your cabin will notice the window that's not quite rectangular, that wall that's not quite plumb, or that notch that doesn't quite fit. You, however, will notice it for the rest of your life. By way of consolation, remember that logs are neither perfectly straight, nor perfectly round, nor perfectly square. In fact, you soon discover that they, like all organic objects, are not perfectly anything. Therefore, do not expect to improve much upon nature and build something consistently straight, round, or square. You're building a home, not a precision watch. Consider the imperfections to be somewhat like the cracks in fine old leather, and you'll be a happier man and a wiser craftsman.

Hand saws. You will eventually need four: a cross-cut saw, for cutting across the grain; a rip saw, for sawing with the grain; a keyhole saw, for cutting out holes, cutting curves, and sawing jobs where the larger saws won't fit; and a hacksaw, for metal. Buy these new. Second hand saws are usually worn out.

Chalk-line. This is a long string, wound in a case containing colored chalk dust. When it is unwound, pulled tight, and snapped against logs or boards, it leaves an approximately straight line of chalk dust along its stretched position. It's handy for many jobs: flooring, roofing, determining spots to be trimmed along log surfaces, etc.

Lug Hook (See illustration.) You use this tool to lift the end of a heavy log a short distance or to snake logs out of the woods. It takes two people to operate. A device can be improvised using a large pair of ice tongs. It will do the same job as a lug hook.

Froe (See illustration.) If you split your own shakes, a time-consuming but satisfying job, you will need a froe. See *In Harmony With Nature* (Chapter X) on how to use it. Few people would recognize a froe these days and even fewer build them, so you will probably have to build your own.

Cant Hook (See illustration.) This is a key tool, and one of the reasons why one or two persons can move very large logs. If you are ambitious and are planning to use large and long logs, this tool will enable you to handle them with surprising ease. Get two, if you can. For work with large logs, try to borrow a dependable hand winch.

If you are planning to put your cabin on a concrete or stone and masonry foundation (which I strongly recommend) you will need the following cement tools: two trowels, one large and one small, a garden hoe, a cement shovel, a few old expendable buckets or similar con-

An axe with both blades curved, to facilitate hand grooving of logs in chinkless work.

tainers, and a tin box for mixing cement and mortar. You can easily make a mixing box with some pounded-flat corrugated roof metal, two boards, and a few nails. A wheelbarrow will be useful in cement and other work.

These miscellaneous tools have special uses or are used infrequently:

Punch: an eight-inch, flat-ended punch is used to drive spikes into pre-drilled oversized holes. *Staple gun and tin snips:* especially useful for installation of tar paper and flashing on the roof. *Vise:* I labored and cursed for two summers without one. The few times you will need it, you will really need it. *Mitre-box and saw:* this equipment is very handy for finish work and enables you to make square or 45° cuts in small wood pieces quickly and accurately. You can make your own mitre-box. *Cables, chain, and rope:* you will need these at various times for various jobs, particularly if you have to drag your logs very far. You'll need some hooks for the chain and cable ends, and need to know a few secure knots for the rope. Inspect the rope and cable frequently and carefully. *Ladders:* you should have a short (six-foot) sturdy stepladder and a long (16-18 foot) ladder. Ladders are expensive, but you can build the long one yourself in about twenty minutes. *Socket set, various wrenches, screwdrivers, etc.:* These will find a multitude of uses, for plumbing, maintenance and finish work, repairing your pickup, etc., etc.

Stairs built from poles, half-poles, and quarter-poles.

10

Your Working Library

In those days, when my hands were much
employed, I read but little ...
—HENRY DAVID THOREAU

There are those among you to whom a log cabin actually *means* working easily in perfect weather until early evening, then eating a delicious meal, lighting the fire, and sitting down to a fat, illuminating book until the wee hours arrive—a splendid conception, the stuff of dreams which does not melt away over the years. You will have these days, to be sure, but not, perhaps, as many as you anticipate. Be not deluded. For one thing, it is difficult to read for very long by candle or lantern light. For another, while you are building your cabin, you will be pretty damned tired by early evening. Finally, you will begin to enjoy your work as much as your reading. You will find the building of the cabin itself an illuminating experience. But on those days that are too wet to work, and when you have tired of tramping about in the woods, you will inevitably turn to your library.

It contains, of course, your favorite books, and those which you've been trying to get to for years. It should also contain several books to help you with your work.

Unfortunately, there are but a handful of log cabin books currently in print and they are sometimes hard to obtain. No single book, including this one, clarifies *all* aspects of log construction. Most of them furnish you with enough basic information to enable you to build your home with the instructions they provide. But if your home is to be an extension of yourself, a uniquely personal architectural expression, you owe it to yourself to look through several books, for if you study the experiences and techniques of several authors, you will develop a methodology which best suits your particular situation and your own nature. And that, after all, is the point of building your own home.

So plan ahead, provide yourself with a working library, and supplement the ideas in this book with those in the books listed below.

Building a Log House in Alaska. Cooperative Extension Service, University of Alaska, 1914 (Revised 1971). 75 pp. $1.00. Available from Cooperative Extension Service, University of Alaska, Fairbanks, Alaska, 99701.

This booklet is crammed with useful information and is universally regarded as one of the best available log cabin publications. It is also a tremendous bargain: 25¢ for Alaskans, $1.00 for out-of-staters. The booklet is richly illustrated and provides in the appendix technical information on insulation and maximum load data that are not included in other books. Additional sources of information for the reader are furnished on the last page. NOTE: The booklet has apparently never been copyrighted, so some of the information, and many of the illustrations and photographs have been reproduced and reprinted in other small pamphlets which are then sold at rip-off prices. So get the original *Building a Log House in Alaska* and look through it before you buy any other small log cabin pamphlets.

In Harmony With Nature. C. Bruyere and R. Inwood. 1975. $6.95 paperback. Available from Drake Publishers, Inc. 381 Park Avenue South, New York, New York, 10016.

If you could only have one other book, it should be this one. It is clearly and exquisitely illustrated. While the book does not deal exclusively with log construction, its authors discuss many fine points which most log books ignore, and which often puzzle the novice. There are sections, for instance, on moving logs into position, using gin poles and hoists, and on sharpening chain saw teeth for "ripping." There is a detailed section on splitting your own shakes. *In Harmony With Nature* will be useful at nearly every stage of construction of your cabin.

Building With Logs. B. Allan Mackie. 1971. 76 pp. $7.50 paperback. For copies, write to B. Allan Mackie, P. O. Box 1205, Prince George, British Columbia, Canada V2L 4V3.

This book, published by a Canadian, is small, but its few pages furnish the reader with the basic steps required to build a "chinkless" log home. Mackie and his associates have founded a log-building school in Prince George, British Columbia, publish an annual magazine (see below), and are keeping the log-building tradition alive and well in Canada's West. Mackie's general approach is rather dogmatic, but his treatment of joist and rafter installation is exceptionally clear, and he provides detailed instructions for hewing the dovetail notch. The book is outrageously expensive, but worth the expense, particularly for beginners.

The Foxfire Book - I. B. E. Wiggington (Ed.) 1972. 384 pp. $3.95 paperback. Available from Anchor Books, Doubleday & Co., Inc., Garden City, New York.

Written by high school students, *The Foxfire Book* contains a long and well-illustrated section on log cabin building. The instructions are thoughtfully divided into categories to suit either the builder who wishes to reproduce a crafted cabin, using traditional tools, or the builder who is interested in a less complicated, but perfectly functional cabin. Details of rafter, joist, and sill and plate log design, which are frequently glossed over in other books, are carefully explained in this very useful book. The authors are careful not to force the designs they have studied upon the reader, and have arranged their recommendation in such a way as to permit the reader to exercise his own creative skills.

The Wilderness Cabin. C. Rutstrum. 1961. 194 pp. $1.95 paperback. Available from The Macmillan Company, 866 Third Avenue, New York, N.Y. 10022.

This book addresses itself to construction of frame and adobe cabins, as well as log cabins, and so does not describe log construction in great detail. But the basic methods are explained, and the author has included clear explanations of several basic operations the log builder will need to learn. *The Wilderness Cabin* will help you to learn how to mix cement, square a foundation, install joists quickly, flash chimneys, etc., etc.

How to Build and Furnish a Log Cabin. W. B. Hunt. 1939 (reissued 1974). 166 pp. $3.95 paperback. Available from The Macmillan Co., 866 Third Avenue, New York, N.Y. 10022.

About half of this book is devoted to cabin construction; the other half to the construction (from poles) of rustic furniture, various fixtures, gates, and fences. The use of traditional tools and methods is stressed. Most of the standard log techniques are included, but in scanty detail. Hunt's recommendations for door and window frames are simple and clear, and result in attractive final products. This is one of the few books which describes methods of building additions onto log structures, a tricky structural and visual problem.

One Man's Wilderness. S. Keith. 1973. 75 pp. $7.95. Copies available from Alaska Northwest Publishing Co., Box 4-EEE, Anchorage, Alaska, 99509.

This unusual book is hard to obtain outside Alaska, and its many color photographs make it an expensive purchase. The book consists of photographs and entries from the journal of an older man who, in 1968, built his own cabin in the deep bush-country of Alaska. It is not intended to be a how-to-do-it book, but the journal entries and accompanying photographs provide vivid blueprints for any reader who wishes to build, with only hand tools, a small, beautiful, and adequate cabin in deep wilderness. The builder, Richard Proenekke, was able to overcome his early misgivings and to transform into reality the dream he shares with many: to live for awhile in a remote wilderness, amidst steep, massive peaks, in the company of undisturbed wildlife.

Log Cabin Construction. J. D. Dunfield. 1974. 90 pp. $5.95 paperback. To obtain copies, write to J. D. Dunfield, 3333 Southgate Road, Ottawa, Canada K1V 7Y3.

Another Canadian publication, this booklet deals only with log work. The author furnishes most of the standard instructions for basic log work (except scribing) and includes many tips that novice log builders will find useful. The most valuable section of this booklet is the appendix, which includes information on numbers and sizes of logs required for different sized cabins, material lists and costs, and labor requirements. If you study these lists and tables carefully, you will be able to accurately estimate your own requirements for building materials well before you begin construction.

How to Build Your Home in the Woods. B. Angier. 1957. 310 pp. $2.95 paperback. Hart Publishing Co., 710 Broadway, New York, N.Y.

This exuberantly-written book covers a wide variety of rustic construction, from cabins to door latches, but few details are provided. Therefore, the book is more useful as a source of ideas than as a construction guide that will help you to solve specific problems.

There are a number of older log cabin books that offer limited help to the beginner. Most of them are now out of print, but they can occasionally be found in libraries. They vary widely in philosophy and usefulness.

Shelters, Shacks, and Shanties. D. C. Beard. 1914. Chas. Scribner's Sons, Inc., New York. 243 pp.

The Real Log Cabin. C. D. Aldrich. 1938. The Macmillan Co., New York. 278 pp.

Your Cabin in the Woods. C. Meineche. 1945. Foster and Stewart Publishing Co., Buffalo, New York. 187 pp.

Log Cabins. W. Swanson. 1948. The Macmillan Co., New York. 207 pp.

Other publications:

Cabins and Vacation Homes. 128 pp. $1.95 paperback. Available from Lane Books, Menlo Park, Calif.

Most of the designs in this book are for frame construction. There is a brief and incomplete section on log work, but the book has useful sections on site selection, spring development, and lumber grades and dimensions. It is inexpensive and useful as an idea source for interior finish work.

The Canadian Log House. $5.00. For copies, write P. O. Box 1205, Prince George, British Columbia, Canada V2L 4V3.

This is a magazine published each spring, which includes log house floor plans, historical pieces on log structures, suggestions for special log installations, and an assortment of stories by and about people who are building log cabins. The second issue points out that the world's largest log building, a 186-bedroom hotel near Montreal, Quebec, was built in 1930 in just four months! Of course, 3,500 log builders worked on it.

*Your Engineered House.*Rex Roberts. 1964. 237 pp. $4.95 paperback. Available from J. P. Lippincott Co., East Washington Square, Philadelphia, Pa. 19105.

This provocative book does not deal with log construction at all, but rather with general principles of heat, light, ventilation, acoustics, and functional design in post and beam construction. The principles can usually be applied to log structures. *Your Engineered House* is of particular value to those persons who have no experience in designing and building, and are looking for an approach to their own cabin design. The author's treatment of doors, windows, and placement of rooms is particularly useful.

We'll consider now several other types of publications which do not deal specifically with construction, but which you are likely to find useful and instructive.

Building a cabin with your hands forces you to slow down. Even if you work very hard and very fast, you will eventually stop to rest. And then you will begin to attend closely to your surroundings. You will wonder about the flowers in that sunny spot, or the new ones that have appeared in the soil you've disturbed. You will eventually wonder about the trees which furnished your logs, and where they grow, and if they love moisture and shade, or heat and sunshine. Have your library stocked with a few field guides to local flora and fauna, so that when this happens, you will be able to feed your growing curiosity. You may have to dig to find guides to the flora and fauna of your particular locale, but they are around. Botanists and zoologists are a curious and busy lot and they've been everywhere. Try the nearest college or university, or nearby state, provincial, or national park. You will be able to obtain from them either general or highly technical guides to the biota of your area.

The Forest Service, Bureau of Land Management, and State and/or County extension services will have local offices which will contribute generously to your working library. These agencies provide information on local flora and fauna, farming and ranching practices, local maps, etc. The U.S. Government Printing Office (Public Documents Dept., Washington, D.C. 20402) will send a free biweekly list of selected publications to anyone who requests it. They will also send you indices of publications by subject area upon request. From these sources you can establish, free or at very low cost, a section in your library on specialized information: plumbing, alternative energy sources, stone and masonry techniques, fireplace construction, spring development and water supply, waste disposal systems, etc.

No one can tell you how to find your land. The land search is a chore which will sorely try your patience and will exact a stiff tax on your optimism. Summon up all of your resolve, for you will curse your fellow man's avarice and learn that "real estate" really means "profit." You may be lucky enough to find something right away. "Luck," however, usually consists of very hard efforts to be in the right place at the right time..You have a precious few things going for you. Prices for isolated parcels of land are still relatively low, although the market is quickly awakening to the fact that isolation has cash value. Look for homesteads which have been abandoned or sold for taxes. Try for land which is marginal or sub-marginal for farming or ranching or land which has had too much energy squeezed from it. You may be able to buy it at a reasonable price and nurse it back to health. If you act soon and if you perservere, you will find something that meets your needs, and on that day the frustration will be swept away in a euphoric flood.

Several recent books contain short sections in which you will find some prudent suggestions intended to help you in your land search and in making your purchase. Browse through them before you buy:

How to Make it on the Land. R. Cohan. 1972. Prentice-Hall, Inc., Englewood Cliffs, New Jersey.

The Homesteader's Handbook. J. Churchill. 1974. 224 pp. $2.95 paperback. Random House, Inc., 457 Hahn Rd., Westminster, Md., 21157.

Homesteading. P. Crawford. 1975. 198 pp. The Macmillan Co., 866 Third Avenue, New York, N.Y. 10022.

The People's Guide to Country Real Estate. J. Young. 1973. 192 pp. $3.95 paperback. Praeger Publishers, 111 Fourth Avenue, New York, N.Y. 10033.

The Complete Homesteading Book. D. Robinson. 1974. 249 pp. $4.95 paperback. Garden Way Publishing Co., Charlotte, Vt. 05445.

Buying Country Property. H. Moral. 1972. 167 pp.

$3.00 paperback. Bantam Books. 666 Fifth Avenue, New York, N.Y. 10019.

The Manual of Practical Homesteading. J. Vivian. 1975. 340 pp. Rodale Press. 33 E. Minor Street, Emmaus, Pa. 18049.

You are not likely to need or have time for much more than the publications listed in this chapter. If you are the bookish sort, and have accumulated a large library, you would be wise to store the bulk of it somewhere until you move into your cabin, for you, like Thoreau, will read but little, and most of your books will just get in the way and take up space you need for other things. When you do find time to read, you will probably find yourself reading about, of all things, your work.

11

Outbuildings

When you first contemplate building a log cabin, the cabin itself occupies, naturally enough, your entire attention. It is easy to forget that there will be other buildings to put up. These other buildings are the subject of this chapter. We'll call them outbuildings.

The cabin will be the main building, and your activities will be centered there, but before you begin work give careful consideration to the various outbuildings you may need as support structures for the cabin itself. Their uses and locations should be planned for, not added as afterthoughts. Decide early what functions you want them to have, for they may affect the design of your main cabin. If, for example, a sauna or sweat lodge is a must, you might decide to put it in a smaller, separate building. In that case, you would not need a large, elaborate bathroom in the cabin, and could use that space for something else.

Once you have decided what outbuildings to put up, you will be able to gather materials for them at the same time you are scrounging for the main cabin. Use of the same style and materials both for your cabin and for its supporting structures will promote a harmonious, integrated appearance, and prevent the outbuildings from looking as if they were built from scraps. Furthermore, if you have designed them carefully, you will be able to earmark and stockpile building materials left over from the cabin construction. If you cut several three-foot sections of log out of your cabin wall for a door space and remember that you need such sections for a part of your sauna, they will wind up stored away, rather than cut up for your wood stove.

An important use of outbuildings is to provide useful structures on which you can practice your log work. If you build them with small logs or poles which you peel, scribe, and notch, you will begin to get the feel, on a small scale, of the tasks which the main cabin will require of you. In miniature, you will learn how to make the building corners square, lay log walls evenly, fit adjoining logs snugly, hew accurate notches, etc.

Another important use of outbuildings is to provide yourself and your tools with temporary shelter while you are building the cabin. You can, of course, move up to the site, put up a tepee or large tent quickly, and go right to work on the cabin. But if time allows, you can build a more substantial temporary shelter to live in until you move into the cabin. When that happy day arrives, you then quickly convert your former shelter into some outbuilding you will need.

What outbuildings could you possibly need? How about these: springbox, well house, outhouse, sauna/sweat lodge, woodshed, barn, stable, chicken house, storehouse, greenhouse, temporary living quarters, root cellar, guest house, workshop, icehouse, doghouse. It's a formidable list, and makes your cabin begin to seem like the keep of the castle or the manor house of the country estate. But each outbuilding on the list potentially satisfies some important need. You may have few of these requirements, especially if you will only be living at your cabin during part of the year, or you may require even more. Your life style and location, present or anticipated, determines what your needs will be. If you don't have electricity and are not willing to give up fresh milk, you must make provision for cold, or at least cool storage. The space for that particular need has to be provided somewhere and should be planned for. Shall it be in the cabin or in an outbuilding?

The list of outbuildings above is somewhat deceiving, for many of the individual functions they serve can, with a little thought, be combined under a single roof. Alternatively, the main cabin can be designed to ac-

A small, simple, and comfortable log guesthouse. The cabin is chinked with molding.

Above: Woodshed. Below, left: A log outhouse blends well with its surroundings and with the main cabin. Below, right: Pumphouse. Note stockade door.

Goat stable of logs and poles.

commodate some needs and eliminate the necessity for some outbuildings. If, for example, you are acquisitive, and have huge piles of junk you can't bear to part with, you either build a storage shed or design some permanent storage space into your cabin. The only other alternative, apart from getting rid of your bulkiest possessions, is to live amidst them in your living room, kitchen, and bedroom.

The needs served by these various outbuildings fall into categories which you will recognize as genuinely essential: food, water, fuel, waste disposal, cleanliness, and storage.

Food outbuildings

Greenhouse. If you are not willing to give up a garden, and yet must live in the mountains, with short growing seasons and sudden frosts, you will need a greenhouse, as well as horticultural skill beyond measure. Greenhouses seem to be difficult to integrate visually with other structures. When attached to frame houses, they usually have a tacked-on appearance. But even as separate buildings, they startle the eye. If you manage to solve this architectural problem, please let me know. If you build an animal shelter, perhaps one end can be successfully used as a greenhouse. Such a location is functionally sound, for manure is handy and the animals' body heat will help the greenhouse to perform its function.

Animal shelters (chicken coop, rabbit hutch, stable, etc.). In the mountains, it is easier to provide your own meat products than your own produce. You could design space for such animals into your cabin. Peasants around the world have put domestic animals in separate quarters, but under the same roof as themselves, for cen-

A goat-stable. Functional and attractive work with peeled poles.

turies. You should, however, obtain domestic animals only after the most careful and honest deliberation. If you have never kept domestic animals, you may learn to your dismay what farmers and ranchers have known since the dawn of animal husbandry: domestic animals require almost constant care and attention. Somebody has to be around nearly all the time, and that somebody is nearly always you.

Root cellar and icehouse. These two outbuildings perform similar functions: preserving perishable foods. Both require a considerable amount of labor—the root cellar because lots of dirt has to be excavated, the icehouse because ice must be hauled in the winter, and because the walls and roof must be thick to provide adequate insulation. I did not build an icehouse because the only recently-built one I have seen did not work. The ice in it was gone by mid-July. I did, however, build a small root cellar directly under my cabin, accessible by a trap door in the living room floor. It is extremely useful.

Springbox. If you are lucky enough to have a spring which runs clear and cold all year, you can reduce the need for outbuildings for storage of perishables. By building a large enough box for storage and by insulat-

ing the box, you can provide an efficient, permanent cold storage unit. Some foods can go directly into the water; others are best stored in the cool space above the water.

Water supply

Springbox. Although I have also included this structure in the food outbuilding section, the main function of a springbox is protection of your drinking water supply. It can be very small if it is not used for food storage. A good springbox insulates the spring source or catch basin for your water and keeps rodents, insects, and grazing animals out of your drinking water.

Well house. This structure performs the same function as the springbox, but will usually double as cold storage space.

Fuel Storage

Woodshed. If you live in an area subject to deep snow, you will have to store an entire winter's supply of firewood and protect it from rain and snow. A winter's supply of wood, if it is your sole fuel source for heating and cooking, is a *lot* of wood. You will need to collect about fifteen to twenty cords of evergreen softwood—the exact amount dependent upon the efficiency of your stoves and cabin insulation, the length of your winter, your elevation, and your personal comfort threshold. A cord is a stacked pile of wood 8′ by 4′ by 4′. You would need a barn-sized building to store twenty cords of wood under cover, but only the chopped, dried wood needs to be sheltered. You can chop and store more wood as you use it in the winter. You will nevertheless need a simple, but fairly large structure. When you fill it, be sure to leave enough room to chop wood inside, so that you, too, will be sheltered from the weather. If you lack electricity, you will have kerosene or gas lanterns. These fuels should be stored in the woodshed or some other outbuilding, *not* in the cabin.

Waste disposal

The Outhouse. Unless you plan to compost human waste, dig a deep pit a fair distance from the house and well away from water. Keep a pleasant view in mind when selecting a location. Don't hide a well-built outhouse. A log outhouse is an attractive little building. The dirt you excavate from the pit should be hauled away or spread around and covered with topsoil. Otherwise the pile of infertile subsoil will lie bare and exposed for years. The outhouse should be far enough from the cabin to prevent an odor or contamination problem, but close enough to run to on a cold, snowy night.

Cleanliness

Sauna/Sweat lodge. If your hygienic or philosophical habits require steam, consider a separate, specially designed structure. Sudden temperature changes and moisture are not good for most soft woods, and might cause problems in the main cabin. An outbuilding, carefully vented and built with cedar, if available, will bear up well to dampness and heat.

Temporary shelter, storage of equipment and people

Eventually, you will have lots of guests. If you are gregarious and tolerate company well, you will design space for them in your cabin. If, however, you must have some privacy during the day or night, build a small guesthouse. You will also eventually have lots of tools and equipment to store. And you may find that you need a workshop. Plan ahead, and you can easily convert your temporary shelter into a guest unit, storehouse, workshop, or the suitable combination of these that your priorities require. Your workshop or guesthouse should contain a heating stove.

Your general strategy with respect to outbuildings should take the following points into account:

Doghouse.

Be realistic. Build only those outbuildings which service activities you will have sufficient time and energy to pursue.

Keep outbuildings to a minimum by combining their functions and designing them into the cabin where possible.

Put them up in order of greatest priority. Obviously, you will need adequate waste disposal and water facilities right away. The chicken coop can wait.

Integrate them visually and spatially with the cabin.

The governing principle here is maintenance and survival. Proper outbuildings are constituents of an integrated life support system, not superfluous frills.

The place to improve the world is first in one's
own heart and head and hands, and then
work outward from there.
—ROBERT PERSIG

12

Getting Ready to Build

In theory, the building task is a culmination of all the thinking and preparation which have preceded it—a simple matter of procedure. You have read through your working library and already know *how* to build the cabin before you pick up an axe. Building it is now merely a matter of placing the logs in their proper positions in correct order, more or less like Lincoln Logs. Then you put the roof on, install the doors and windows, and move in.

In practice, of course, the process is a good deal more complicated. Some steps will require more time than you had anticipated, others less. Poor weather may slow you down. A sliced thumb will inhibit your notching for a few days. There will be quite a few unexpected events which will slow down your progress, but not many that will speed it up.

As much as I would like to avoid telling you how to build your cabin, I cannot refrain from offering some strategies for speeding up your work and avoiding unnecessary complications. They are offered as suggestions for your consideration, not as rigid procedural rules, since dogma is as counterproductive in log cabin construction as in any other creative endeavor.

The objective of this section is not to tell you, 1-2-3, A-B-C, how to build, but rather to provide you with some idea of how much time and effort to anticipate for various stages of construction, how many procedural options are available to you, and where to find specific information you may need.

Before cabin construction begins:

If you spend nearly as much time and effort in preparation as in construction, you will probably solve many problems before they arise. Have enough of your stone materials at the site to get started on foundation work. Have your lumber at the site, sorted and stacked. Have your tools repaired, sharpened, ready to go. The exact cabin site is selected. Your working library is handy, your books well thumbed through, and your pickup is running well. Windows and doors, already built, are piled somewhere out of the way, sheltered from dust and rain. Your logs are either neatly stacked nearby or will arrive soon. The sun's shining. It's a fine day to begin.

se-fitting round notches require careful, patient axe-work.

13

The Foundation

For this, and all following construction stages, we will assume that you have a road to your site, that you lack electricity, and that you have one strong and faithful helper.

Tools: *hammers, shovels, saws, tape measures, levels, square, trowels, hoe, buckets, mixing box, wheelbarrow, garden hose or transit, pencils.*

Materials: *cement, sand, water, rocks, nails, lumber, twine.*

There are very few jobs involved in building your cabin that are bummers. This—building a solid foundation—is one of them. The job consists essentially of digging holes in the ground, and then carefully filling them back up again. No matter how you plan it, a sturdy foundation will require several days of your time. Holes must be dug, forms built, cement mixed. Each step takes time and is *hard* hand labor. Even after the foundation has been poured, you should wait two or three days for it to harden before you begin laying logs on it.

Foundation work is a good time to have work parties. The key to successfully utilizing the offers of help you receive from friends is to have the proper tools, in sufficient numbers, on hand to keep everyone busy. If you don't have enough tools, somebody will be dawdling around getting bored, then visiting. Pretty soon it's a hassle, and the work slows way down. It's better to have plenty of tools around to keep all hands busy. Then your friends will know that they've really helped you out and have not merely discharged some silly social obligation. We have nearly forgotten that the ancient purpose of most festivals was celebration of the end of a period of

hard work. When you work, work like hell—and when the work's done, celebrate like hell.

Work parties should be carefully planned, with preliminary work done, tools lined up, tasks assigned, etc. You'll have to supervise the work carefully, and make sure that each helper understands clearly what he or she is supposed to do. Directions get crossed up easily when lots of people are working fast and helping each other.

When starting construction on your cabin, your major options are to put the structure directly on the ground, to build a continuous foundation for it (see illustration), to set it on wooden posts (see illustration), or concrete or masonry piers (see illustration). If you set your cabin directly on the ground, the lower logs will soon rot, so forget about that option.

A continuous foundation is the sturdiest permanent foundation you can provide. It cannot be surpassed for strong support and for keeping the lower part of the cabin insulated. There are some serious objections, however, to continuous foundations. Because they run the full length and breadth of the cabin, a great deal of digging is required, even for a small cabin, and all that dirt you dig up has to be carried off somewhere. A continuous foundation also requires a lot of concrete, which means lots of cement, clean sand and gravel, and water. This means frequent trips to the building supply store for cement, to the gravel pit for sand and gravel (which must be nearly free of organic matter), and to the creek for water. The cement will probably have to be mixed in small batches, so you will have to pour the foundation one section at a time. If you do this, you can build forms for each section, then take them down when the concrete has set, and re-use them for the next section. Otherwise, you must build forms for the entire foundation. Either method is time-consuming. Finally,

Above, left: The builder used a combination of poles and dimension lumber for his porch support system. Right: Stone and masonry piers. The house is chinked with pole quarter-rounds and caulked with asphalt-base sealer.

Below, left: A fine example of a continuous stone and masonry foundation. Both foundation and log work were done by the same craftsman. Right: Note that the first sill log set onto the foundation is cut in half lengthwise.

Above: The relatively lightweight enclosed porch is supported with stone and masonry piers. Note the use of vertical logs between the windows.

a plain concrete foundation does not look very good under a log cabin. Cement blocks look even worse (see illustration). You can improve the looks if you face the concrete foundation with native stone. Most people who build their own concrete foundations intend to do this eventually, but it seldom seems to get done. In general, a continuous foundation is fine, but it will cost you dearly in hard labor, time, and money.

Your third option is to set your cabin on wooden posts, or concrete, or stone and masonry piers. Treated wood posts are the quickest to put up. You dig the holes, put the posts in, align and level them, firmly tamp them in (no easy job), and you're ready to go. However, no matter what kind of wood they are or what kind of preservative they are treated with, they will eventually rot. If you are in a moist climate, they decompose sur-

prisingly fast. Some builders minimize this problem by setting treated wooden posts on top of small concrete footings. (See illustrations.) But since you have to dig holes anyway, you might as well use concrete or stone and masonry piers, which will last for generations, and do not require much more effort to install. Concrete or cement blocks go up fast, but again you face the visual problem. That leaves stone and masonry.

Go out and look at some foundations just to see what's around. You will find only a few foundations built up of native stone, but I'm sure you will find these to be the most attractive. (See illustrations.) Not many are seen these days because of the time and labor involved in their construction and because it is commonly supposed that only a stonemason can build them. If you choose, however, to use stone and masonry piers, you can cut time, labor, and cost drastically, compared to building a continuous foundation, while providing appealing supports for your cabin. You can easily build the piers using mortar and local rock. It takes some practice to find the right consistency for the mortar and to fit the rocks together in a pleasing pattern but, if you start out with the piers that will not be visible, such as those under the center of your cabin, by the time you build the last pier, they will be symmetrical and sturdy-looking. This style of foundation doesn't require much cement, but it does take lots of rock and clean sand.

How many piers? That depends upon the size of your cabin. My thirty by thirty cabin, with a full length eight-foot wide porch, took fourteen piers. The support provided is more than adequate. Put an old piece of steel reinforcing rod or some similar metal scrap in the top of each pier such that it sticks up about five or six inches. These fit holes drilled in the plate logs, and secure the logs to the piers.

How deep should the piers be buried? This depends upon the type of soil at your site and how well drained it is. Most books advise burying piers down to frost-line. The theory is that if you sink them to a level above the frost-line, they will shift as the ground freezes and thaws, and thus will not provide solid support for your cabin. I was horrified to learn that the soil froze at times to a depth of nearly six feet at my own site, but soon learned that none of the residents in the area ever buried their foundations deeper than four feet, and had never had foundation problems. So if you are in doubt, ask the old timers in your locale for advice.

If you are building on permafrost, you have special problems, for which you should consult *Building a Log House in Alaska.*

Whichever type of foundation you decide on, there are three key operations involved: mixing concrete and mortar properly, getting the foundation corners square, and getting the foundation level.

Mixing concrete and mortar—If you can find an old piece of corrugated sheet metal without holes in it, you can pound it flat and make yourself a mixing boat nearly free (Figure 1). With something like a hoe, thoroughly

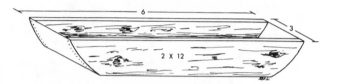

Figure 1.

dry-mix materials for both concrete and mortar in this container before adding any water. For concrete, use one shovelful of cement to six shovelsful of clean gravel, or if you have clean sand available, one shovel cement to two shovels sand to three shovels of gravel (no rocks bigger than about 1½″ in the gravel). Add water a little at a time, and mix until the mixture is thoroughly moistened, without grey streaks of cement, and just runny enough to assume the shape of the form into which you will put it. Don't add more water than necessary. It makes the mixing easier, but it also makes the concrete weaker. I warned you that this was hard work. You can add clean, wet rocks as fillers in the foundation, but be sure they are surrounded by concrete.

To mix mortar for brickwork, concrete blocks and stonework, use the following proportions: one part cement, three parts clean sand, one-tenth part hydrated lime. Follow the same routine as with concrete—first dry-mix, then add water, a little at a time, while you mix it. You want a mixture which is thoroughly moistened, yet thick enough to adhere to the brick or stone or wall and to firmly support it. If you add too much water, the mortar is weakened, and it runs all over the place. I'd suggest that you experiment with small batches until you can get the consistency right for the material with which you're working.

There are several methods for laying out your foundation and squaring corners. I will illustrate one method. For more information, see the following books:

In Harmony With Nature. Bruyere and Inwood.

Building With Logs. B. Allan Mackie.

Wood-Frame House Construction. L. O. Anderson. 1970. Agriculture Handbook No. 73. $2.25 paperback. Available from Supt. of Documents, U.S. Government Printing Office, Washington, D.C. 20402.

First, pound a stake in at one of the corners (A). Three feet from that stake, pound in another (B). Now put in stake C, at a right angle and four feet from stake A. *If* the distance between stakes B and C is five feet, you have a square corner. If the corner is not square, adjust stake C until the distances are as indicated in the diagram, and you'll eventually get it squared. Now, by measuring from stake A, put stakes in the other three corners of the house. Don't put them in permanently, because you will be making finer adjustments later.

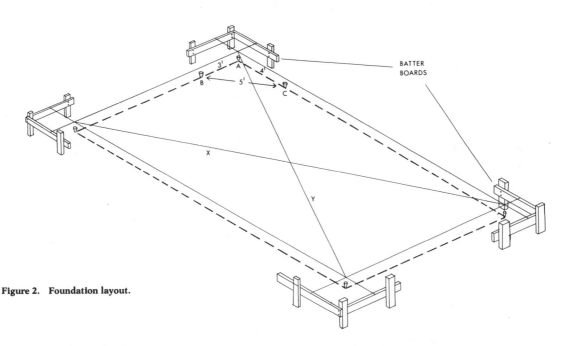

Figure 2. Foundation layout.

Study the diagram in Figure 2. You want the centers of the first four logs you put into place to lay in the positions represented by the *dashed* lines. Whatever type of foundation you put in must therefore furnish support along or at points on that line. Your problem is to ensure that the corners are square.

Next, put in the batter board stakes. These should be put in firmly, so they can't be easily knocked out of position. They should be placed at least four feet from your corner stakes.

How high should the batter boards be? Decide how high you want your foundation supports to be, and then nail in the batter boards so that their tops are as high as your foundation will be. By this means, you will later be able to use the batter boards to check on horizontal as well as vertical alignment of your foundation. If you follow this suggestion, you must make sure that the batter boards are level. This is easy if you have a surveying instrument called a transit or level. They are horribly

much hose you'll need. Now look at Figure 3. At corner ⋅A, nail the batter board to the stakes at the height you wish the foundation to be all around the house. Then tape or tie one end of the hose to the batter board at corner A, and have your partner take the other end to one of the other corners and hold it at the approximately correct level. Then fill the hose with water—no big bubbles in the hose, please. When the water level at

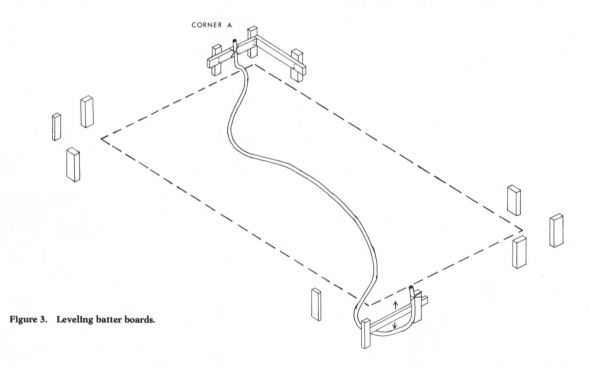

CORNER A

Figure 3.   Leveling batter boards.

expensive, so you probably don't have one. Neither do I. There is another way, as usual. It's a hassle and can't be done alone, but it works.

Scrounge some plastic hose which is sufficiently transparent to enable you to see the water level inside the hose. Measure the *diagonal* distance between your corner posts and add a couple of feet to determine how

your end is even with the batter board at corner A, your partner can put the batter board at his end into position. Have him nail it into place and double-check. If the water levels at both ends of the hose are even with both batter boards, they are level. Repeat the process at the other two corners.

Now that the batter boards are in place and level, back

to squaring the corners, and back to Figure 2. String some good heavy twine over the batter boards so that they intersect directly over your temporary corner stakes. Use a plumb bob if necessary. Now measure the length of the diagonals, X and Y. If they are equal, the building is square. They probably won't be, in which case your cabin is a parallelogram instead of a rectangle, so keep adjusting the twine until you can measure equal diagonals.

When you get the building square, adjust the corner stakes and pound them in firmly. If you are going to use posts or piers, place stakes for these into position as well. Now carefully mark the position of the twine on each batter board, move the twine over, and make a shallow saw cut into each board where the twine was. Saw cuts are better than pencil marks, which always seem to disappear when you need them most.

Now you can move the twine out of your way while you excavate the foundation, but replace it quickly and accurately when needed. The job's done.

This builder has spliced his sill logs (left) in order to use short log sections. He is filling in the gaps between concrete piers with stone and masonry to provide a continuous foundation.

14

Walls and Floor

The foundation, we assume, is finished. Now what?

First, let's get oriented. We need a common structural vocabulary, so look over Figure 4. Refer to the glossary for definitions of structural features not illustrated in Figure 4.

A bewildering variety of options for walls and floor are available to you, but since every cabin book insists on its own formula for success, how do you choose among the options you are offered? The only way is to consider each of the major possibilities individually, see how it strikes your intuition, balance that off against the time and effort required, and *then* decide. To assist you, I have compiled below most of the major options you are likely to choose from, along with their respective advantages and disadvantages.

Tools: *hammers, crowbar, chain saw, hand saws, axes, hatchet, files, draw knives, log dogs, scribe, pens and pencils, chisels, brace and bits, tape measures, level, square, chalk line, cant hook, punch, cables, chain, rope, ladders.*

Materials: *lumber, logs, nails and spikes, poles, roll insulation, thirty-pound insulated felt.*

As you can see, this stage of construction requires most of your tools. You won't need too many different materials, but large quantities of each.

Since you've just experienced the tedious chore of building the foundation, it's a shame that you're immediately faced with another rather dull, laborious task: peeling your logs. It's necessary, however, for if you leave the bark on, you provide prime habitat for innumerable wood-boring insects and termites, and all manner of bacteria and fungi. So peel the bark off with your draw knife or peeling spud. It's fun—at first. If your logs are dry, this may be the single most time-consuming operation your cabin involves. Apart from moving dirt, it raises the most sweat. Some builders recommend peeling your logs immediately after you fall the trees. It is true that if you do fall your logs in the Spring, when the sap is "up," the bark is much easier to peel. But there are some serious objections. First, if they are peeled and allowed to sit for several months, they may discolor badly, and that burnished golden hue you've looked forward to may be replaced by grey and black splotching. Second, if you have to move a peeled log very far to your cabin site, it usually arrives full of gouges, scratches, and ground-in dirt. For these reasons, I recommend that you endure the blisters and aching muscles, and peel the logs at your site. It is to your advantage to have all of your logs peeled before you begin to put them up: you will then know the exact sizes of your logs, and can sort them accordingly. Log-peeling is an excellent central theme for a work party. That's why you need two draw knives (more if you can find them). Take heart, though, for once this particular job is completed, you have passed a major milestone.

Once you grasp the use of the scribe and gain some skill with your axe, laying-up logs goes fast. A long day may see one or more complete rounds of logs laid up, even for a large cabin with interior log walls. A smaller cabin will, of course, grow higher even faster. You will eventually be able to scribe, saw, and hew out a notch at a log intersection in ten to twenty minutes (round notch). The logs fairly fly up to their proper position. The end of each day brings new exhiliration, for the cabin is growing, as bread dough rises, nearly before your eyes.

Installation of floor joists will require considerable time—several days—if you use poles for joists and mortise them into the sill logs. Several operations are

Wall logs, with a vertical notch for installation of the door frame spline.

involved in the installation of pole joists. They must be peeled and both ends squared. One side must be worked to form a flat surface on which floor boards can be nailed firmly. Finally, the sill logs must be accurately notched to receive the squared ends of the joists (Figure 5A). Adjusting pole floor joists so that their straight surfaces are all even with each other (to provide a flat floor) and uniformly on the same plane (to provide a level floor) is

Figure 4.   Schematic log cabin section. Dashed lines indicate portions of the tie log and wall logs which will have to be trimmed to accommodate roof eave. Grooves in the edges of door and window openings will receive splined window and door frames, a design feature which allows wall legs to settle unimpeded around the openings.

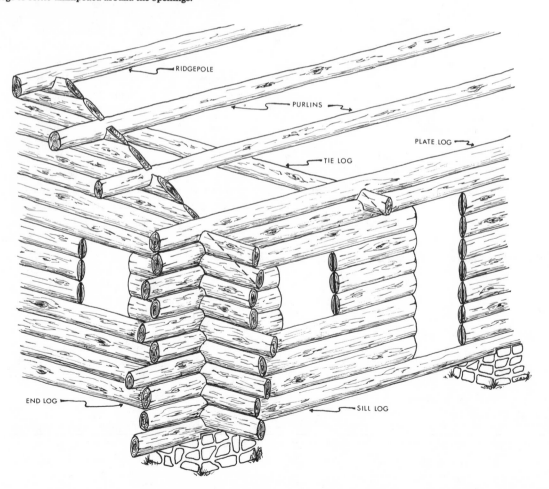

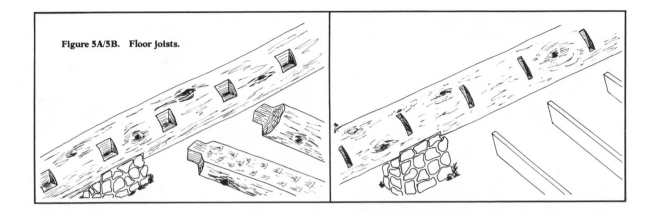

Figure 5A/5B. Floor joists.

tricky and requires care and patience. Installation of rafters—and of ceiling joists, if necessary—requires somewhat similar time-consuming attention.

Let us now consider the options at this stage of construction.

As you lay up successive rounds of logs, you may fit them closely and tightly as you go, or you may leave spaces between logs for the moment, to be filled when you chink and caulk later on. If you have selected your logs with great care, they will fit tightly, requiring only slight effort to trim high spots or flatten irregularities. But if the logs are severely tapered, bowed, or knobby, achieving a close fit is hard, frustrating, and time-consuming work. It can be dangerous as well, if a log high above the ground must be repeatedly turned, hewed upon, and canted back into position to check for fit. The temptation is to leave whatever gaps result from poorly notched logs and chink them later. The end product, with careful chinking, will be adequate, weathertight, and relatively durable. It will not look bad when the walls are finished. But it may remind you for years that you might have done a better job. It is far better to spend more time finding good logs than closing gaps resulting from poor building material.

Some builders advise hewing or sawing a groove the length of each log, which will fit down snugly over the upper surface of the log under it (see illustration). A

Heavy floor joists rest directly on a cement block continuous foundation and are placed in slots cut from a three-sided log. The same principle can be used in working with round logs.

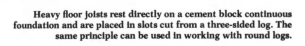

Above, left: A fine example of "chinkless" notching. This is only the second cabin this builder has erected. Above, right: After scribing, the wide V-shaped notch is cut out roughly with a chain saw, then finished with axes to closely fit the lower log.

Below: Large-log chinkless construction in an unfinished home. Note the use of purlins outside of walls (for roof overhang) and the thick, insulated roof. The four log ends at center are the joists for the cabin's loft.

strip of insulation is stuffed into the groove and notches, so that when the log is rolled into place the insulation is pressed down onto the log beneath it. Cutting out such a groove with gouge chisel, axe, or adze is an exacting, slow job, but a shallow V-shaped groove can be quickly cut with a chain saw and then touched up with the axe. Careful scribing and axe work using this method produces an excellent fit. This technique has the added advantage of reducing checking (longitudinal splitting) in your logs as they dry. Further, as the logs settle over the years, they are not likely to shift position laterally. This method of log construction is usually referred to as "chinkless." It will, of course, take longer to lay up logs using this method. On the other hand, you will not have to spend time chinking later on. Its beauty and durability recommend it highly. (See illustrations for examples of chinkless construction.)

There are two good reasons for placing insulation between your logs as you go, whatever method you use. First, you will never be able to get insulation or other chinking materials quite as tightly into place as when you are laying the logs. The pressure exerted by the logs in the wall holds the materials firmly into place. Second, if you should fall behind schedule, and the first snowfalls force you to move into your cabin before it is completed, the insulation you have placed between well-fitted logs will provide weather-tight protection for you through the Winter.

You have about a dozen different notches to choose from (see illustrations). They range from the traditional dovetail, which requires considerable skill, to flat notches which can be done very quickly with a chain saw but which make the corners look rather like stacked building blocks. My own preference is for the round notch, sometimes mistakenly called a saddle notch. It seems to be a happy compromise between the difficult dovetail and the unesthetic flat notch both in terms of the time and skill required, and the simple grace it lends to cabin corners is unexcelled.

Above: The round notch is very difficult to scribe and hew when used for log walls which do not intersect at right angles. Below: Dovetail notching in a recently built cabin. The art is not extinct.

Above: The classic round notch and corner. Note the bench constructed of poles and half-logs. Below, left: Large-log chinkless construction. Note the use of half-poles in the window frames. The corner is chinked with polyurethane foam. Below, center: End-on view of excellent recent dovetail notchwork. Below, right: Unusual designs often require unusually shaped notch work. Such notches are time-consuming, but attractive.

Above: Notches are avoided altogether in this design. The cabin will be chinked with mortar. Below, left: This type of corner allows for very rapid construction. Cedar strips are used for chinking in many Canadian cabins. Below, right: This type of corner notch allows for rapid wall construction. Note pole floor joists notched into sill log. A log cabin need not be built with large logs. Seventeen six to eight-inch diameter logs form each wall of this cabin.

The pointed ends on the pole rafters and the trimmed edges of the wall log ends give a robust, rough-hewn look to this home. Note the curved window frame.

There are also several corner styles you can choose among, some of which eliminate altogether the necessity to notch your logs (see illustrations).

Most cabin books advise you to lay down wall logs so that their sides are vertically plumb on the inside surface of the wall. This arrangement will lend a straight, even look to the walls inside your cabin, but there are some disadvantages to this technique which you should be aware of. While it provides symmetry to one side, it merely accentuates asymmetry on the other, so that there is no net improvement in the wall's appearance. More important, if your logs vary much in diameter, they will not balance well while you are working on them when aligned in this fashion. Since logs must be firmly dogged into position for scribing, trimming, etc., under the stress of increasing weight from above the smaller logs may actually be pinched out of their proper position and dislodged. A better method of alignment, especially if you are working with sharply tapered logs, is to place the logs with their centers, not their sides, in vertical alignment. The logs will balance in such a position with only minimal support while you work on them, and in the finished wall they will appear to be in natural repose (Figure 6).

Shall you have interior log walls? Such walls mean more peeling, more notches, more chinking. The cabin will go up more slowly. But they also provide beauty, structural and thermal utility, and the sense of wholeness which a one-room shelter usually lacks. By all means provide for interior walls in your design, and provide adequate foundations for them, for unlike frame interior walls, log walls are heavy. They will cost you more construction time, but not very much more, because some of them will be shorter than the outside walls and the shorter logs will be easier to handle and fit together. The extra time invested is far outweighed by the utility gained. Interior walls allow more efficient heat, noise, and people control, and open a variety of structural possibilities: lofts, ceilings, second floors,

additional support for purlins, ridgepoles, etc. You might well consider positioning interior walls so that one end of your cabin is open and spacious—simply one large space—divided by an interior wall from a smaller, cosier, ceilinged space. Such a design combines the pleasant space that openness provides with the warmth and security of smaller rooms.

As soon as you begin to lay logs, two more options demand immediate attention: how do you plan for your doors and windows and when do you build your fireplace?

For doors and windows you may either place short sections of logs on either side of window and door openings you have planned for, or you may lay wall-length logs into place and cut out the openings later. There are two advantages to using short sections of logs. First, the total number of logs you will need for your cabin is reduced, though not by much. Second, it is easier to handle the shorter, lighter sections, an important con-

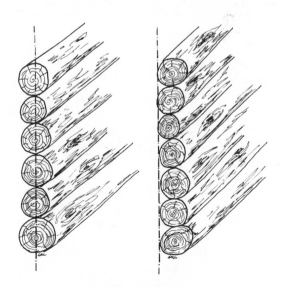

Figure 6.   Log alignment.

The vertical notch in the ends of the wall logs allows for the installation of a spline to which the door frame will be attached. The spline holds the logs in place, yet allows them to settle unimpeded.

sideration if you are working alone. This method, however, takes more time, and more important, does not allow for changing your mind later. If you put the entire log up and cut out the openings later, you will have had a chance to get the feel of the space your cabin provides, and will be able, if necessary, to shift the positions of doors and windows from their originally planned locations. If you decide on this method, which I heartily recommend, you should spike the wall logs to each other about two feet back from both sides of the contemplated door or window opening as each round is laid up, so that the logs will not shift under their own weight between the time you cut the openings and install the door or window frames. Be sure to mark the locations of the spikes clearly, for if you hit one in the morning with the chain saw, the rest of the day will be spent repairing the chain.

If you cut out window and door openings after the wall logs are in place there will be a short period during which your cabin will resemble a solid log fortress. You will soon tire of climbing over the walls to get in and out of the cabin, and your neighbors will chide you for building a frontier stockade, but once the plate logs are set into place, all the openings can be cut and framed at once, and your stockade will suddenly and dramatically begin to look like a home.

Plan ahead when you cut out the openings. Make sure, for instance, that your wood stove will fit through the door. Measure your windows and doors, homemade or storebought, sketch out your window and door designs, and *then* cut out the openings to their proper size.

Everybody wants a fireplace in their cabin, despite the fact that they are costly in time and effort, inefficient as heating devices, voracious consumers of hard-earned firewood, and are apt to turn your cabin into a smokehouse if they are improperly constructed. You probably want one, too. So do I. Someday . . .

But it is important that you realize that a handsome, properly built fireplace requires great skill, patience, and thought (see illustrations). If you design your cabin with the fireplace providing structural support for walls, purlins, or rafters, you have no choice but to build the fireplace as you build the cabin. This involves mastering the skills of fireplace masonry as well as the skills of log construction all at once. Progress on the cabin will be slow and you will be tempted to do a hasty job on the fireplace. A well-crafted hand-built fireplace deserves plenty of time, not a rush job treatment. A large fireplace can take as much time to build as the cabin itself, so think carefully and read widely before you decide to construct your cabin and fireplace simultaneously.

But if you must build your cabin quickly—remember that the snow flies early in the mountains—I advise you to put in the foundation for your fireplace, build your cabin around it, and install the fireplace later, at your

The cobblestone foundation motif is continued in the chimney. The house is chinked with mortar.

creative leisure (see illustration). Such a procedure requires careful planning, and may eliminate some fireplace styles as options for you. If you plan ahead, you can position roof supports in such a manner that they will not obstruct the installation of a large stone and masonry flue at some later date. In the meantime, the fireplace foundation you have installed will serve well as a solid, fireproof base for a pot belly stove, or if you must have an open fire, a Franklin-type fireplace.

Soon after the foundation is completed and the first round of logs is in place, you must attend to your cabin's floor. How shall you support it, and what type of floor shall it be? If you use poles for floor joists (see illustration), you save a considerable amount of money,

Below, left: This chimney seems to flow through the purlins and roof. Below, right: Note the space left for the fireplace installation. The highest two wall logs have been cut to allow for eventual chimney construction. The walls will be chinked with pole quarter-rounds. Note the halved sill log.

Log superstructure for a two-story post and beam house. Note the notches at the top ends of the vertical logs and the floor joist construction.

but as mentioned above you will invest considerable time in their proper installation. Since the floor joists are hidden from view, I recommend the use of dimension lumber if you can afford it (Figure 6B). There are better jobs than this one in which to invest so much time (see illustrations).

In order to keep your cabin efficiently heated, you should seriously consider insulating your floor. This means a double floor (subfloor and finish floor), more time and more lumber, and more expense for insulating materials. But it is very nearly a necessity if you will be in winter residence at your cabin. I have lived in both

insulated and uninsulated cabins in severe winters and from experience I earnestly recommend that you insulate both floor and roof of your cabin. The extra time you take to insulate them as you build will be returned to you several times over in saved firewood during the years that follow.

The finish floor is a matter of taste, of what is available, and of what you can afford. Hard- or softwood tongue-in-groove flooring complements the log walls beautifully, but is expensive and time-consuming to install. It is also difficult to smooth evenly without the use of an electric sander. A host of other flooring materials,

Above, left: The horizontal log at the center of the photograph ties opposite walls together and also provides support for a roof truss. The short log which underlies it provides additional support. Above, right: An attractive and strong log roof truss. Note the heavy rafters.

cheap and expensive, are possible choices for your finish floor.

As your log walls near completion, another series of options present themselves: Tie logs or not? A second floor or loft? Or neither? Ceilings or open-beam construction? What sort of gables?

A tie log is a brace which connects two walls to provide lateral support for both (see illustration). The walls are usually described as "tied together," which does not quite convey the rigidity of the connecting member. A short log wall, say up to sixteen feet or so, is usually quite firm, with the notches at either end furnishing sufficient support to prevent lateral movement. But when a continuous log wall reaches twenty-five feet or longer, it may shake slightly about halfway between the corner notches, simply because over that distance the logs will flex under stress. (How shaky the wall is depends partly on how well the notches are fitted and how large the logs are.) Go to the center of your longest continuous wall and at about eye level put all your weight on the wall and try to shake it back and forth. If you can just barely move it, it is not necessary to tie it to another wall. If it shakes easily, moving an inch or more from center, you would be wise to install a tie log, perhaps two. Tie logs can be simply ornamental, when they are not really needed, or structural, when they are required. They often support roof trusses. The best installations combine both functions. They should be notched fairly high into the walls they support, well

above your head. They should be carefully selected for appearance, for they appear to float across a living room space above your head, and inevitably draw attention to themselves. For the same reason, their placement is important: seek to install a tie log or logs to divide space symmetrically (see illustrations).

Second floor? Loft? I strongly recommend that some sort of second level be considered. The problem is in deciding what kind.

A loft is a second story in which you bump your head a lot. This is not to say that you should choose between a full second story and nothing, but merely a recognition of things as they usually are. How you design a loft depends entirely upon what you intend to use it for, now or in the future. If you intend to sleep there, you should provide it with ventilation, for it can become a heat-trap, an oven, both in summer and winter. If it is to be a studio, workshop-hideaway, den, or serve some purpose that requires light and space for moving about, provide adequate head room and windows or you will find yourself avoiding it. If you really intend to spend a lot of time there, consider a full second story. If your loft is for storage only, most of these problems disappear.

Let's assume that you want to store some things in the loft, as well as provide sleeping space for guests, and perhaps do some work up there once in a while. In this case you might consider putting a loft over one-half to one-third of your main floor space. This amount of loft area will provide considerably more living space, *if you* put an extra two or three rounds of logs above the joists for your loft's floor (see illustration). Why those extra two or three rounds? First, they provide just enough extra head space to make the loft comfortable to move around in. Second, they provide for abundant storage space adjacent to the wall, leaving the center of the loft—under the ridgepole—free for beds, desks, tables,

etc. Third, they will lend the portion of the cabin which is not under the loft a feeling of luxurious spaciousness.

A full second story is a major undertaking; a cramped loft, full of acute angles, is not good for much besides storage. The expanded loft seems to me to be the ideal compromise. With the investment of about two days' extra work you will construct a multi-purpose area

Below: Note that three rounds of logs have been placed above the ceiling joists to provide for a roomy loft.

joists. It would be faster and easier to use dimension lumber than to use poles for support. But here, peeled poles notched into the plate logs are exceptionally appealing, while dimension lumber, though certainly not unattractive, is rather prosaic. The same choice will face you with respect to exposed rafters. What shall they be? Two-by-fours (or two-by-sixes) or peeled poles? The two-by-fours go up quickly and are easy to handle. The peeled poles require time and tinkering. The only way to make an informed choice here is to find cabins built both ways and to decide for yourself which you find most attractive.

Before you begin to build the roof, you must decide on what style of gable to build. The classic log gable is favored (see illustrations), but many builders substitute frame gables, frequently built with attractively weath-

which will add appreciably to your living space, without uncomfortably diminishing your cabin's roominess.

If you decide to put a loft in your cabin, you must put in joists to support its floor. These, unlike the floor joists, will be exposed (see illustration). The same construction situation obtains with these joists as with floor

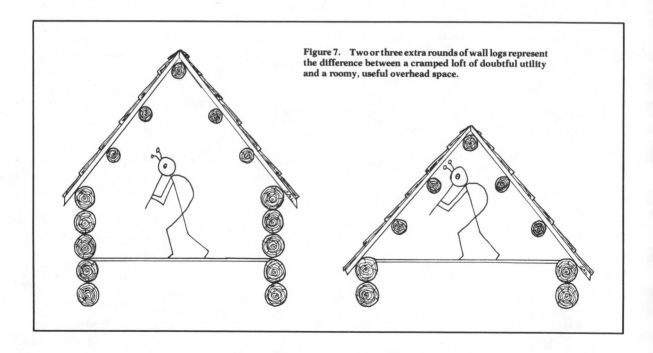

Figure 7.   Two or three extra rounds of wall logs represent the difference between a cramped loft of doubtful utility and a roomy, useful overhead space.

Compare the following features of these two cabins: gable style, corner style and notching, porch and roof support systems (both use purlin/rafter/ridgepole, but the cabin at left uses dimension lumber rafters and purlins, while the other uses pole purlins and rafters).

The installation of purlins in this house is generous in order to sustain heavy snow loads. The horizontal lines of the house are pleasantly interrupted by the palisade sections around the windows.

A "classic" log home design, with shaked roof and gables and a dormer window.

ered wood or faced with shakes. The log gable takes somewhat longer to build than the frame gable, and there are difficulties in providing it with lateral support during construction. Windows can be put into either log or frame gables without difficulty. Do not cut the ends of the gable logs to match the roof's pitch until they are all into place and the purlins and ridgepole have been installed.

A final suggestion: As you place your wall logs, stagger the ends which extend beyond the corners. Do not cut off sections which extend unnaturally far beyond the corners unless they are consistently in your way, or unless you must shorten a log in order to handle it. Those projecting log ends will provide secure and well-located supports for the scaffolding you will later need for chinking and caulking work on the outside of your walls and gables. A good rule of thumb is never to cut either end of a log or pole which has been placed into position, unless construction requires that it be shortened immediately or if it creates a hazard. You can always cut it off later, and in the meantime you might discover that you need it for something important.

The key operations—Walls and Floor:

Types of notches and corners. See the photos in this book, and

The Foxfire Book. E. Wiggington (ed.).

How to Build and Furnish a Log Cabin. W. Ben Hunt.

How to Build your Home in the Woods. B. Angier.

Building With Logs. B. Allan Mackie.

Scribing and notching

You will finally learn these skills by doing them rather than reading about them, but to get you started:

Scribing—

The object of scribing is to enable you to fit one log snugly down onto another log. What the scribe does, in effect, is to transfer the exact surface configuration of the lower log to the upper log. The end product of a corner scribing job is an oval, closed, pencil line on the upper log which accurately duplicates the shape, at the corner, of the lower log. Once the line is on the log, you then carefully remove all the wood inside that closed line. If you have scribed accurately, the upper log will then fit down snugly onto the lower log. It sounds easy, and it is easy if you keep the theory firmly in mind.

It is also easy, however, to make mistakes when you're first learning to scribe. The following precautions will eliminate most of them:

1) Keep the points of the scribe perpendicular to each other at all times while you are scribing! To repeat: Keep the points of the scribe perpendicular to each other at all times while you are scribing!

2) Once you have adjusted the scribe, be sure that it is firmly fixed into that position. If it slips open or slips closed while you are scribing, you have to start all over again, or you will fail to achieve a close fit.

3) Don't rush. Relax, take your time, and scribe ac-

The support for this porch is attractive as well as sturdy.

curately. It's a slow job at first, but once you get the hang of it, the work goes quickly.

Scribing and Hewing the Round Notch—

Your two sill logs are in place on your foundation, with their butt ends pointing in opposite directions. You are ready to put up the end logs, which will be the first logs you notch.

The following section describes a method of measuring and hewing out one type of notch—the round notch—using a divider-type scribe. It is a style I happen to prefer, but don't forget that there are other methods, many other notches, and a few other types of scribes.

First, put an end log up on the sill logs, such that its butt rests on the tip end of a sill log. (On each wall, lay successive logs butt to tip, tip to butt, etc.)

From one end, sight along the length of the end log to see which face is smooth, straight, and free from irregularities. When you have selected the most even face, check the side opposite that face for bumps, knobs, etc. The two opposite faces which are smoothest and straightest will be the top and bottom sides of the end log when it is finally notched and set into place. Mark the top and bottom sides on the end of the log, and move it into position at the corner. Make a mark on the side of the sill log directly beneath the center of the end log (Figure 8-A).

Firmly dog both ends of the log into place, top side up (Figure 8-B). Set your scribe open to a distance equal to half the diameter of the end log (Figure 8-C).

Set the scribe so that the top (pencil) point is at the bottom of the end log and the bottom point on the side of the sill log (Figure 8-D). Be sure that the points of the scribe are perpendicular. Now move the scribe upwards and toward the top of the sill log, keeping both points touching the two logs (Figure 8-E). Move the scribe to the top of the sill log, points perpendicular at all times (Figure 8-F). You have now completed one-quarter of the scribe-line.

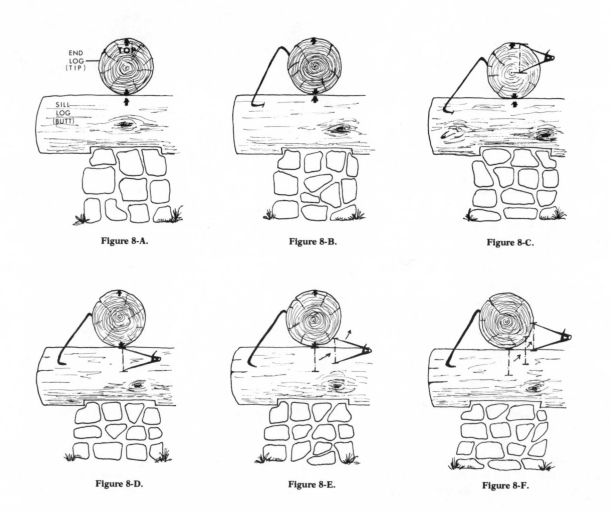

Figure 8-A.

Figure 8-B.

Figure 8-C.

Figure 8-D.

Figure 8-E.

Figure 8-F.

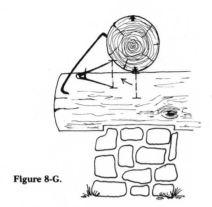

Figure 8-G.

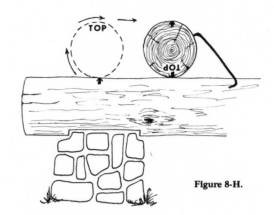

Figure 8-H.

Now move the scribe to the opposite side of the sill log, and repeat the process, starting, as above, with the top (pencil) point of the scribe touching the bottom of the end log and the side of the sill log. When this portion is scribed, half of the scribe-line is completed.

Bring the scribe back to the outside of the sill log and scribe again, this time in the opposite direction of your first scribing (Figure 8-G). Then scribe the remaining quarter-circle of the scribe-line, and the job is completed.

Figure 9 illustrates how the scribe-line should appear from the side. Note that irregularities in the contour of the sill log are duplicated in the scribe-line.

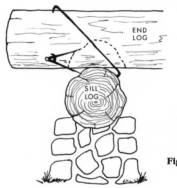

Figure 9.

Before proceeding, check to be sure that the scribe hasn't slipped. See if it is still adjusted to one-half the diameter of the end log (Figure 8-C). Then make sure that your scribe-line is visible. If you have scribed correctly, you will have drawn a continuous, roughly circular pencil line on the underside of the end log.

Next, scribe the notch at the other end of the end log.

When both notches are scribed, take out the log dogs, and roll the end log 180° toward the inside of the house. Dog it into place, bottom side up and top side down (Figure 8-H). Get into the habit of rolling all of your wall logs toward the inside of the house. By doing so, you'll provide yourself with more of the lower logs to sit on while you scribe and notch, and you will also be less likely to accidentally roll a log off the wall. It happens.

Now we'll look at the scribed end log from the top view (Figure 10). Be sure that the scribe line is distinct.

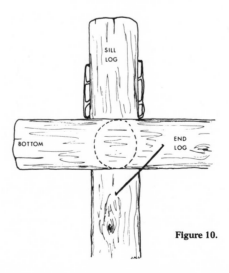

Figure 10.

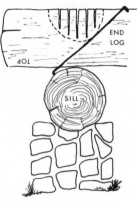

Figure 11-A.

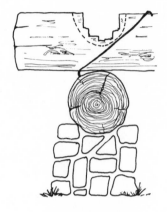

Figure 11-B.

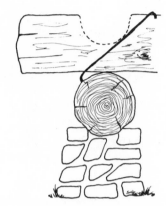

Figure 11-C.

Place the log dogs such that they will be out of the way while you notch the log.

The job is now to remove the wood from inside the scribe-line. You could go right to work on it with chisel and axe. Many craftsmen do just this. But you can speed up the job considerably at no cost in appearance by making several vertical cuts in the notch with the chain saw. Do not cut past the scribe-line (Figure 11-A), but "dish out" the bottom of each cut slightly, to facilitate cupping the notch later on. Then knock out the large blocks of wood with the axe to form the rough notch (Figure 11-B).

Now comes the step, which if executed with care and patience, will result in tightly-fitted, beautiful corners—given accurate scribing. With short, gentle strokes of your sharp axe, follow along the scribe-line trimming away the wood adjacent to it. Don't worry yet about the wood in the middle of the notch. Trim down to the line, but don't trim away the line itself. Slowly and carefully, now. When you have trimmed all the way around the scribe-line, then hew away the excess wood from within the notch, cupping it about an inch deep. The finished notch should have smooth edges and be slightly cupped, with the scribe-line just visible at its edges (Figure 11-C).

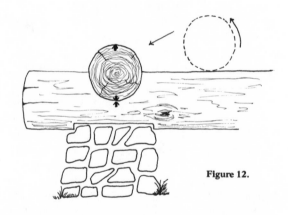

Figure 12.

Next, hew out the notch at the other end of the log.

When both notches are done, take the dogs out and roll the log back over 180° to the corner. Line up the center of the end log with the mark you made on the sill log (Figure 12), and check for fit. If you have worked accurately, both notches will fit snugly down over the sill logs. More likely, despite your best efforts, there will be a few high spots to be trimmed. Mark these spots on both notches, roll the log over, trim them and try again for closer fit.

When you have a good fit, roll the log back over, stuff a layer of fibreglass insulation (or whatever chinking

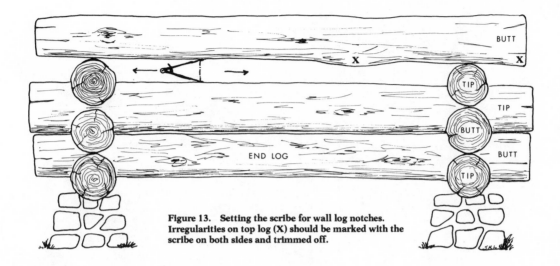

Figure 13.   Setting the scribe for wall log notches. Irregularities on top log (X) should be marked with the scribe on both sides and trimmed off.

Figure 14A/14B.
Shallow and deep notches.

material you have decided upon) into the cupped notches and roll permanently into place. You are now ready to start on the next log, so relax awhile.

If you had ideal wall logs, all with very little taper and nearly identical in size, you could continue to set your scribe to one-half of their diameter as you put them up, and they would fit together as shown in Figure 12. Unfortunately, logs are seldom so uniformly shaped, so after the sill logs and end logs are in place, I recommend that you set the scribe as indicated in Figure 13. Run the scribe along between a wall log already into place and the next one you are ready to install. Set the scribe at the largest average distance between the two logs. Do not set it at narrow spots caused by irregularities in the log (X in Figure 13). These will have to be trimmed off in order to achieve a close fit.

When you have the scribe set, check to see how deep the notches will be at both ends of the log before you begin to scribe. Avoid notches which are too shallow (Figure 14-A) or too deep (Figure 14-B), for these errors tend to be cumulative, and become increasingly difficult to correct as you proceed.

If you find that your next notches will be too shallow, you have three options. First, you can try reversing the log, so that its butt and tip are adjacent to the butt and tip

Two remarkable notches are illustrated here. Wooden wedges can be driven into the slots in the end of the log at upper left, then cut off to produce a very tight joint.

of the log beneath it. Be cautious with this option, however, for it may cause you notching problems on the other walls. Think ahead. Second, you can trim away enough of the lower surface of the troublesome log until it will fit tightly down against the lower log. This is a lot of work, however, and may harm the cabin's appearance. The third and probably best option is to select another log from your stockpile.

If you find that the next notches will be too deep, you have little choice but to select a slightly larger log.

If you have been very particular in your original selection of house logs, and if you keep the effective length of your logs in mind (Chapter VIII), you won't have any of these hassles.

For more information on installation of sill and plate logs, purlins, floor joists, and ceiling joists, see:

In Harmony With Nature. Bruyere and Inwood.

The Foxfire Book. E. Wiggington (ed.).
Building With Logs. B. Allan Mackie.

For more information on types of flooring and their proper installation, see:

Wood Floors for Dwellings, 1961, Agricultural Handbook No. 204, Available for 35¢ from Supt. of Documents, U.S. Government Printing Office, Washington, D.C. 20402.

For pictures and sketches of various designs and floor plans, study the photographs in this book closely, and also see:

The Foxfire Book. E. Wiggington (ed.).
How to Build and Furnish a Log Cabin. W. Ben Hunt.
·The Canadian Log House. P.O. Box 1205, Prince George, B.C.

Close-fitting round notches require careful, patient axe-work.

15

The Roof

Tools: *hammers, knife, staple gun, saws, tin snips, level, axe, hatchet, chalk line, square, tape measures, ladders.*

Materials: *insulation, weather surface materials (shakes, shingles, roll roofing, etc.), roofing tar, nails, tar paper, lumber, flashing, chimney and flue accessories.*

The walls are up, plate logs in place. Fall is in the air, but you are ready to roof your cabin.

You do not have to be a structural engineer to design and build a sturdy roof for your home, though it may seem so at your first consideration. Logs are strong. In most instances, your common sense will inform you correctly. If you are in doubt, study the maximum loading data in Table I, and proceed.

You will, of course have decided how steeply to pitch your roof before you build your gables. Your options are flat, moderate pitch, or steep pitch. Flat roofs present too many problems in snowy country and should normally be avoided. The factors which you should consider when deciding how steeply to pitch your roof are snow load, weather surface materials, appearance, and difficulty of construction. The factors are inter-related.

If you receive very heavy snowfalls, you must either build a steeply pitched roof or remove accumulated snow periodically. In most places, however, a strongly supported, moderately-pitched roof will bear heavy snow loads without danger of collapse.

Pitch determines choice of some materials. Shakes, for instance, will not function properly on low-pitched roofs.

Maximum Loading of Round Beams, Purlins, Rafters, or Joists

DIAMETER (inches)	MOMENT OF INERTIA (IN4)	WEIGHT lb/ft	LOAD (POUNDS/LIN. FT.)								
			SPAN (FEET)								
			8	10	12	14	16	18	20	22	24
6	64	9.8	331	170	98	62	41	29	21	16	12
7	84	13.4	435	223	129	81	54	38	28	21	16
8	201	17.5	1047	536	310	195	131	92	67	50	39
9	322	22.1	1667	859	500	313	210	147	107	81	61
10	491	27.3	2557	1309	758	477	320	225	164	123	95
11	719	33.0	3745	1917	1110	699	468	329	240	180	139
12	1017	39.3	5297	2712	1570	988	662	465	339	255	196

Reprinted by courtesy of Cooperative Extension Service, University of Alaska, Fairbanks, Alaska.

Cedar shakes are most effective on steeply-pitched roofs. This house was built by a man-and-wife team over two years while both were employed full time at other jobs.

An attractive bay window in a chinkless log home. The thick roof is well-insulated.

Appearance is a major consideration. Before you select a steeply pitched roof, I suggest that you go out and find some A-frame houses in the woods and look them over. We are taught that the steep, dramatic lines of the A-frame design are particularly well suited to forest surroundings, that the design complements and reflects the tall, perpendicular lines of the forest. Some find it so; others find the design interruptive and unnatural. Try your own eye out on the A-frame before you decide.

Finally, a steeply pitched roof will require more materials and time for construction because it is larger than a low-pitched roof covering the same area. Special scaffolding must be built to allow you to safely work on it. Log gables may be ruled out for a particularly steep roof. Work on a steep roof is especially difficult if you are working alone, so arrange for some help, if possible.

A variety of materials are available to you for the weather surface: rolled roofing, shakes, asphalt shingles, etc. Shakes are the most attractive, but take longest to install and are expensive to buy. With a tool called a froe, you can split your own shakes, but it is a slow process. A shake roof, like a fireplace, is something of a luxury installation for the first year's work, and is a job that should not be rushed. If, however, you install rolled roofing or asphalt shingles, you may easily overlay them with shakes later, and in the meantime you will have a serviceable and reasonably attractive roof.

Roof installation can go very quickly. Or it can drag on for days or weeks as a result of poor preparation.

Certain aspects of roof construction are weather dependent. In rainy weather, roof support logs or scaffolding may be too slippery for safety. On very cold days, tar-impregnated materials may split easily when you are handling them. It is therefore very important to have all of your materials ready and close at hand, so that when good weather arrives, you can be working on your roof rather than driving to town for materials.

Installation and alignment of the roof's supporting structure—rafters, purlins, ridgepole, gables—involves considerable time, for all of these structural members must be adjusted and readjusted as they are fitted into place. Once this work is done, the roof itself goes up quickly.

The first decision you should make is whether or not to insulate your roof. An insulated roof will more than double the materials required and the time needed to install it, for in effect you must build a double roof, with insulation material sandwiched between (see illustrations). On the positive side, such a roof will keep your cabin cool in summer and warm in winter. In very cold climates, an insulated roof is a necessity; even in moderately cold climates it may make the difference between comfort and severe discomfort. If you are in any doubt about whether or not you really need an insulated roof, err on the side of insulation.

You may choose from three orthodox roof support systems commonly used in log construction. In each system described here, the ridgepole is supported at each end of your house by the frame or log gable. The factors which should determine your choice are the size of your cabin; the snow, wind, and roof material loads you expect your roof to support; the appearance you prefer.

Rafter-ridgepole system (See illustrations.) No purlins are used in this method. A series of rafters are

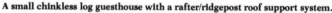

A small chinkless log guesthouse with a rafter/ridgepost roof support system.

Top: Purlin-ridgepole roof construction is illustrated here. The roof is designed to support heavy snow loads, with a pair of purlins installed between each gable log. Note palisade sections and use of quarter-logs for door frame. Above: This builder has wisely selected straight logs with very little taper for his purlins. Note the plate log just above the door, the ridgepole, and the classic log gable.

supported by the plate log at the lower ends and by the ridgepole at the upper ends. The roof itself rests on the rafters. This system is fine for small cabins, but is inadequate for larger homes which have longer spans between plate logs and ridgepole—especially if the roof pitch is moderate or low.

Purlin-ridgepole system (See illustrations.) No rafters are used in this system. Instead, the roof rests directly on the purlins. Expected loads and the horizontal span determine how many purlins are installed. Some builders characteristically install a pair of purlins between each gable log. If the purlins must span great distances and are small in diameter, they may require support with roof trusses, columns, etc. Table I will tell you how much weight you can expect a log purlin of a given diameter to support over a given distance.

Purlin-rafter-ridgepole system (See illustration.) This system makes use of all three structural members. The purlins support the rafters, which in turn support the roof. The same structural precautions obtain with this system as for the purlin-ridgepole system.

Various combinations of the systems, making use of tie logs, columns, trusses, and other structural members are possible.

Minor points.

When you install purlins, rafters, ridgepole, etc., do not forget to allow for a substantial overhang for scaffold support, and later, for eaves.

Take particular care to seal the joints where the roof joins the sill logs, atop the walls, and along the upper edges of the gables. You would be well-advised to chink and caulk these joints as you build the roof, even before you have started to chink and caulk the walls, because the wall-roof joints are often hard to reach after the roof has been installed.

Be especially careful to fireproof your chimney, flue, and stovepipe installations. *This point can not be overemphasized!* Virtually every log builder advises extreme care with respect to chimney and flue installation, yet every year hundreds of cabins burn because of faulty or careless stovepipe fireproofing.

Reference for key operations—roof and gables.

Roof support designs:

Building a Log House in Alaska. University of Alaska.
Building With Logs. B. Allan Mackie.
The Foxfire Book. E. Wiggington (ed.).
Log Cabin Construction. J. Dunfield

Insulating materials:

Building a Log House in Alaska. University of Alaska.

Above, right: The rafters outside of the walls allow for the roof overhang. Note the deeply grooved log at lower left.
Below: A simple, effective porch design.

16

Chinking, Caulking And Sealing

These operations are intended, of course, to weatherproof and preserve your cabin. The best jobs will not only perform this function, but will also contribute to your cabin's beauty. Poor chinking, on the other hand, is not only unsightly, but will require constant maintenance.

Both chinking and caulking are time-consuming, particularly if wide gaps have been left between wall logs, or if your logs are very knobby. In your planning, keep in mind that the chinkless method of log-building nearly eliminates an entire stage of construction. At the chinking stage, you will recover much of the extra time you spent in grooving the logs as you laid them up. Remember, *both* sides of the walls must be chinked.

The tools required depend upon the chinking and caulking materials you select.

CHINKING

I have visited recently constructed homes and cabins chinked with cedar strips, pole quarter rounds (peeled and unpeeled), mortar, moldings of various shapes, small round poles, oakum, clay, moss, fibreglass insulation, and even polyurethane foam. There is little point in trying to assign an order of preference for these materials. The various builders employed them in accordance with such divergent factors as appearance, cost, availability, familiarity with the material, and comfort threshold. Some builders like to hermetically seal their cabins, while others like to see through the walls. Both builder-types seem happy with their own style of chinking. Here are some of the advantages and disadvantages of various chinking materials:

Cedar (or other split wood) strips can be installed very quickly, compared to other materials and the rough wood is attractive. But the chinking itself is neither rodent-, nor insect-, nor waterproof. (See illustrations.)

Pole quarter rounds are, as the name suggests, quarter sections of poles. Do not try to cut these by hand or you'll be years getting done. Use a chain saw or find someone with a large circular saw and cut your poles lengthwise yourself. I prefer to use peeled poles, but unpeeled quarter rounds provide an interesting visual contrast with peeled logs. The dried bark may, however, shelter wood-boring insects. Quarter rounds are usually form-fitted to the logs adjoining them with careful axe-work. Long sections (to 14 or more feet) may

A two-story octagonal log house. The building is chinked with cedar strips.

Above, left: These remarkable stairs are made from one large log. The house is chinked with quarter-rounds and caulked with asphalt-base sealer. Right: An imaginative roof design. The house is chinked with unpeeled pole quarter-rounds.

often be fitted into place since green quarter rounds flex appreciably, so cut long poles. If the edges of the quarter rounds are caulked, the walls will be waterproof and nearly air-tight. (See illustrations.)

Mortar chinking is form-fitting, since it is semi-solid when applied. The problems involved are designing means to keep it firmly in place, and preventing it from cracking as it dries. The mortar will stain your logs if carelessly applied. Despite these problems, mortar chinking is an effective sealant, and is favored by many builders. (See illustrations.)

Moldings of several different shapes are used for chinking. Their sealing characteristics are about the same as cedar strips, if not caulked. Some types of moldings are quite expensive, so price them and go to work with pencil and paper before you buy. (See illustrations.)

Small round poles are used for chinking infrequently, for although they go up fast, they are hard to work with. They do not weatherproof a wall unless they are caulked as well.

Oakum, which is tar-impregnated hemp or jute, is used to caulk the seams of wooden boat hulls, and also works for cabins. It expands when damp, and so is an effective sealant. It can be hammered tightly into the crevice between logs, but should then be covered with

some other material. It is moderately expensive.

Moss. In these days of fractional distillation and complex plastics chemistry, there are still builders who use moss for chinking. It is often put into notches and grooves in chinkless building. Dry sphagnum moss is

Mortar chinking.

preferred. Its chief advantages: it is free, and it absorbs many times its weight of water, and so will keep out the rain.

Fiberglass insulation is more frequently used in chinkless construction or is wedged between logs and covered with some other material. It is used to minimize heat loss by infiltration. In construction other than chinkless style, it is used along with some other chinking material, such as quarter rounds. (See illustration.)

Polyurethane foam is a tight-sealing chinking material, but has several practical disadvantages. It must be painted or stained, it is expensive, and it must be applied with special machinery. Another negative factor—it may produce very toxic fumes if it catches fire. (See illustrations.)

There are, then, lots of ways to chink a cabin. The best way for you to select your own style is to look at as many different styles as you can find. You may have to travel around some, for chinking (and notching) styles tend to be concentrated regionally.

Some general notes on chinking: Anticipate a long, somewhat tedious job with chinking, no matter what material you decide upon. Consider chinking parties. Always use long, galvanized nails to attach your chinking materials. The galvanized nails will hold better than plain nails, and will not rust-streak your chinking for many years. Finally—as I have suggested earlier—consider avoiding chinking altogether by grooving your logs. (See illustrations.) If you do decide to chink, experiment with several methods until you find the material that best suits your taste, time, and labor requirements.

Reference material on chinking:

How to Build and Furnish a Log Cabin. W. Ben Hunt. (contains mortar formula).

How to Build your Home in the Woods. B. Angier. (contains mortar formula).

Building a Log House in Alaska. University of Alaska.

Reference material on chinkless construction:

Building With Logs. B. Allan Mackie.

Building a Log House in Alaska. University of Alaska.

The corner is chinked with polyurethane foam.

CAULKING

Caulking is the final step in making your cabin weathertight. Even if you build a chinkless home, you will need to caulk between roof and wall, foundation and walls, and around doors and windows.

Several types of caulking compounds are marketed. Look for a material which is waterproof and which maintains its elasticity. Compounds which can be applied with a caulking gun will enable you to do a neater and faster job than those which must be applied with a trowel. Asphalt-base compounds, which are black, are favored by most builders, but plastic-base white or cream-colored compounds are also attractive, particularly in interiors.

SEALING

One major job remains: application of oils and sealers to the logs. Let's consider first what an ideal sealer should accomplish.

You want a substance which will preserve the logs' rich color, or which will achieve the precise hue you desire. It should seal in pitch and resinous materials, and protect the wood by deterring the penetration of bacteria and fungi. It should be cheap, easy to apply, and not malodorous.

No product I know will meet all of these criteria, but several approach them. Untreated logs will darken with exposure, and many builders favor this naturally-seasoned appearance. There is, however, strong evidence that treatment will appreciably increase the serviceable life of a log.

Although no sealant is perfect, there are some steps you can take to increase any sealer's effectiveness. Apply preservatives after the wood is fully seasoned. The logs will darken slightly during this period, but the sealer will be absorbed better by dry logs than by green logs. As you build, remove noticeable infections of stain and mold from the log's surface in order to minimize later development of decay in the interior of the log. Since the cellular structure of wood allows for greater longitudinal than lateral penetration of bacterial infection, be especially generous in applying sealer to the cut ends of your logs. For maximum effectiveness, plan on resealing your logs every five to seven years. With such treatment, a house will be nearly impervious to decay organisms.

Exterior sealants

Several brands of clear urethane finishes are available which will preserve for years the light colors which characterize newly-built cabins. These are fire-retardants, and will reduce the tendency of logs to turn grey with exposure. The finishes are not themselves fungicides.

The active ingredient in most fungicidal solutions is pentachlorophenol, usually called "penta." It is readily available in farming and ranching areas. Penta may be added to most commercial sealers, but it will darken the logs somewhat, depending upon how much is used.

Here is the mixture which has been used successfully for decades by the Forest Service to protect their own log structures: two quarts of boiled linseed oil, 1½ cups penta, and one quart paint thinner.

Boiled linseed oil and another commercial preparation, logwood oil, are favored by many builders. They are expensive, however, and do darken with age. Builders who prefer dark logs and who delight in bargains

apply used crankcase oil to the exterior log surfaces. It is brushed on lightly, allowed to soak in for a day or two, and then the excess is wiped off. New crankcase oil does not darken the logs so much as used oil, but both tend to collect dust.

Interior sealants:

Your guiding principle for interior surfaces should be to maintain coloration, to offset the tendency of cabin interiors to be somewhat dark. Since the interior will not be exposed to moisture, shellacs and varnishes may be used. Most builders apply a coat of shellac to the logs, followed with one or two coats of a flat, matte-finish varnish.

If you want a deep, shiny finish on your logs—especially attractive on purlins, rafters, built-ins—apply several coats of marine spar varnish, sanding lightly between coats. It is expensive, but results in an especially lustrous finish.

Three general suggestions with respect to log treatment will help you to avoid most problems. First, check around in your area to see what other log builders have used, and see for yourself how various treatments are working in relation to the moisture and sunshine regime of your specific locale. A treatment effective in one area may not be effective elsewhere. Second, protect your skin and eyes when using any substance through direct contact. Finally, test all finishes on a short section of peeled pole before you buy. Most paint stores will let you test several types before selecting one. If they gripe about it, find another paint store. Keeping in mind that penta is a darkening agent, mix a few small batches of various concentrations and try them out on your test pole before mixing up the final batch for the cabin.

No log books with which I am acquainted provide much information on this subject. It is not a very critical step, but if you want to go into it in scientific detail, you can obtain the following publication for a quarter: *Preserving Wood by Brush, Dip, and Short-Soak Methods*, A. F. Verrall, 1965, Technical Bulletin No. 1334, Forest Service, U.S. Dept. of Agriculture. Available from Supt. of Documents, U.S. Government Printing Office, Washington, D.C. 20402.

17

Finish Work

If you are like most first-time log builders, you will want to trim your house with log or pole products, and if you have time, to build your own interior structural fixtures from the same products.

Why?

First, you will have discovered through your construction experience with the cabin itself that logs are both sturdy and tractable. The wood will assume whatever shape your care and patience dictate. Balustrade work illustrates the point. (See illustrations.)

Second, you will realize that logs and poles are cheap, and your budget is getting tattered.

Finally, you will have begun to suspect that anything you build into your cabin which is not hand-crafted will detract ever so slightly from the structural, indeed architectural harmony your cabin has assumed. The cabin is exerting its magic.

Staircases, bookshelves, woodboxes, counter supports, cabinets and cupboards, door and window frames, mantles and hearth trims, all manner of built-ins

Left, above: Simple and beautiful lines make this new porch a handsome addition to an older log structure. Left, below: This porch was added to an older log building. The cabin purlins provide support for the added porch. Below: A simple porch design.

have taxed the ingenuity of scores of log builders. Much of their interior log work and trim is as clever as it is beautiful.

The photographs in this book will provide you with a few ideas, but the subject is too large and too important to treat with justice here. A future book will deal with it in detail.

Finish work requires, above all, time. Your cabin will teach you that all the world's money won't speed up by much those jobs which require your steady hand, your judgment, your sense of quality. You may complete your cabin to the extent of moving into it in a summer or two; quality finish work may require the rest of your life to complete.

But then, really, what better way to grow old?

"Your work," as poet Gary Snyder puts it, "is the investigation of a new style of life, and with the exploration of ways to explore your inner realms—with the known dangers of crashing that go with such."

A log planter. The building is chinked with sections of molding.

Glossary

A dormer window of logs.

Balustrade. A railing made up of vertical members (balusters), top rail, and bottom rail, used on the edge of balconies, stairs, etc. (Page 117)

Bay window. Any window space projecting outward from the walls of a building. (Page 108)

Beam. A structural member transversely supporting a load. (Page 49)

Caulking. (Noun or verb.) The material used to stop up and make joints or seams tight against leakage. (Page 113)

Chinking. (Noun or verb.) The material used to fill a chink, such as a strip of wood used to close the crevice between the adjoining logs of a cabin. (Page 96)

Dimension lumber. Wood cut to pieces of specified size.

Dormer. The term given to any window protruding from a roof. (Page 119)

Eaves. The lower border of a roof that overhangs the wall.

Flashing. Sheet metal strips bent to fit wall and roof surfaces, intersecting roof surfaces, or chimneys in order to make watertight joints.

Gable. The vertical triangular portion of the end of a building from the level of the eaves to the ridge of the roof. (Page 97)

Joist. The architectural members which furnish support for the floor (floor joists, sometimes mistakenly called stringers or sleepers) (Pages 83, 87) or for the ceiling (ceiling joists). (Page 95) Usually spaced 16 or 24 inches apart.

Pier. A column of masonry used to support other structural members. (Pages 74, 75)

Pitch. The term used to describe the amount of slope of a roof.

Plate logs. The top wall logs, which furnish support for the lower end of rafters and for ceiling joists, etc. (Page 110)

Purlins. The horizontal logs (or beams) in a roof which are supported at both ends and which support the rafters or roof. (Page 97)

Quarter round. A section from a three to six inch pole that has the cross section of a quarter circle. Used for chinking, window and door trim, molding, etc. (Pages 74, 113)

Rafters. Those structural members which provide support for roof material. Their size depends upon span, weight of roof materials, snow and wind loads. Usually spaced from 16 to 24 inches apart. (Pages 94, 109, 111)

Ridgepole. The highest horizontal log in a roof and the receiver of the upper ends of the rafters. (Pages 109, 110)

Roll roofing. Asphalt-saturated roofing material, supplied in 36-inch wide rolls, each of which covers one square (100 square feet).

Shake. (Noun or verb.) A shingle split from a piece of log, usually two to four feet long. Used for the weather surface of a roof or to face gables, walls, etc. (Page 106)

Sill logs. The lowest wall logs, which rest directly on the foundation and which furnish support for floor joists. (Pages 74, 79)

Spline. A wooden strip that fits into a groove or slot between parts. (Pages 49, 90)

Tie log. A beam, usually one or more logs, which connects and provides lateral support for two opposite walls.

Truss. An assemblage of members typically arranged in a triangle to form a rigid framework that cannot be deformed easily by external force. Usually a roof support structure. (Page 94)

Index

Acknowledgements

I am indebted to my teachers, those craftsmen who utilize the mountains' raw materials with respect and regard—Denny Blouin, Bart Darnell, Gary Giles, Bob Gregg, Lloyd Hahn, Wayne McRory, Henry Meyer II, Henry Meyer III, John Mortenson, Roger and Carolyn Schramm, Chuck Spray, Ben Tolland, Umar, Linda White, John Whittaker, Bodie and Madelaine Wittington—and to those builders I was not fortunate to meet, and those who wish to remain unnamed.

Grateful acknowledgement is made for permission to reprint from the following: THE WILDERNESS CABIN (revised edn.) by Calvin Rutstrum (©Calvin Rutstrum 1961, 1972); HOW TO BUILD AND FURNISH A LOG CABIN (revised edn.) by W. Ben Hunt (© 1974 by Macmillan Publishing Co., Inc. Copyright 1939, 1947 by W. Ben Hunt); HANDMADE: Vanishing Cultures of Europe and the Near East by Drew and Louise Langsner. © 1974 by Drew and Louise Langsner. Used by permission of Crown Publishers, Inc.; LIVING THE GOOD LIFE by Helen and Scott Nearing. Copyright © 1954 by Helen Nearing, Copyright 1970 by Schocken Books, Inc. Reprinted by permission of Schocken Books, Inc. THE FOXFIRE BOOK, 1972, edited by Eliot Wiggington, Copyright © 1968, 1969, 1970, 1971 by the Foxfire Fund, Inc. Reprinted by permission of Doubleday & Co., Inc.; REGARDING WAVE by Gary Snyder. Copyright 1967, 1968, 1969, 1970 by Gary Snyder. Reprinted by permission of the author.